A STUDY OF

Twentieth-Century Harmony

A TREATISE AND GUIDE
FOR THE STUDENT-COMPOSER OF TODAY

Da Capo Press Music Reprint Series

GENERAL EDITOR

FRANK D'ACCONE
University of California at Los Angeles

A STUDY OF

Twentieth-Century Harmony

A TREATISE AND GUIDE
FOR THE STUDENT-COMPOSER OF TODAY

Volume One—HARMONY IN FRANCE TO 1914

by RENÉ LENORMAND

Volume Two—CONTEMPORARY HARMONY

by MOSCO CARNER

DA CAPO PRESS • NEW YORK • 1976

Library of Congress Cataloging in Publication Data

Lenormand, René, 1846-1932.
    A Study of twentieth-century harmony.

    (Da Capo Press music reprint series)
    Translation (v. 1) of Étude sur l'harmonie moderne.
    Reprint of the 1940 (v. 1) and 1942 (v. 2) editions
published by J. Williams, London.
    CONTENTS: v. 1. Harmony in France to 1914.—
v. 2. Contemporary harmony.
    1. Harmony. I. Carner, Mosco. A study of twentieth
-century harmony, v. 2. 1976. II. Title.
MT50.L59A72 1976   781.3'09'04   76-40058
ISBN 0-306-70717-9

This Da Capo Press edition combines Volume One and Volume Two of *A Study
of Twentieth-Century Harmony. Volume One—Harmony in France to 1914* by
René Lenormand is an unabridged republication of the revised edition published
in London in 1940 and is reproduced from an original in the collections of the
UCLA Music Library. *Volume Two—Contemporary Harmony* by Mosco Carner is an
unabridged republication of the first edition published in London in 1942
and is reproduced from an original in the collections of the Memorial Library,
University of Wisconsin.

Published by Da Capo Press, Inc.
A Subsidiary of Plenum Publishing Corporation
227 West 17th Street, New York, N. Y. 10011

NEW EDITION

A STUDY OF
Twentieth-Century Harmony

(ÉTUDE SUR L'HARMONIE MODERNE)

A TREATISE AND GUIDE
FOR THE STUDENT-COMPOSER OF TO-DAY

BY

RENÉ LENORMAND

ENGLISH TRANSLATION BY

HERBERT ANTCLIFFE

With Preface by MOSCO CARNER

Volume One—HARMONY IN FRANCE TO 1914

LONDON: JOSEPH WILLIAMS, LIMITED
29 ENFORD STREET, MARYLEBONE, W.1

U. S. A.

PARIS

THE B. F. WOOD MUSIC CO.
BOSTON

" LE MONDE MUSICAL "
114 *bis* Boulevard Malesherbes

A COMPANION VOLUME
TO
RENÉ LENORMAND'S BOOK

A STUDY OF
Twentieth-Century Harmony
— Volume 2 —

BY
MOSCO CARNER

Contemporary Harmony

READY SHORTLY

☞ *Copies can be ordered of the Publishers* ☜

TABLE OF CONTENTS

INDEX OF MUSICAL EXAMPLES

PREFACE TO THE NEW EDITION

THIS book first came out under the title "A Study of Modern Harmony." The facts, however, that it was written before the Great War (1914-1918), and is in the Author's own words "almost exclusively French in its scope" seemed to demand the adoption of a new title for the present republication, a title more precisely describing its actual scope. Thus the choice fell upon "Harmony in France to 1914."

French harmony of this period is essentially that of the so-called impressionistic composers with Debussy as their central figure. It is late in the day to stress again in detail the important place which the harmonic style of this school occupies in the evolution of modern harmony, not only in France but in other countries. During the first decade or so of our century there was hardly a musical nation in Europe—and this applies also to a great number of composers in North and South America—that was not in varying degrees influenced by the French impressionists. It was the last occasion in the history of music that the individual style of a national school was so generally accepted in other countries.

A complete technical study of musical impressionism in France would have, of course, to include a number of phenomena besides harmony. Nevertheless, harmony is unquestionably the most interesting aspect of impressionism. For although the ground was already prepared on the one hand by the later German romantics, notably Wagner, and on the other hand by some of the Russian writers of the nineteenth century, the harmonic inventions and changes of the French impressionists were so many and so far-reaching that they imperatively demand special and separate study.

A few words about the Author and his method. René Lenormand (1846-1932) belonged to the same generation as Fauré, Chabrier and Duparc. He was primarily known as a song writer and composer of chamber music. He also founded and directed the society *Le Lied en Tous Pays* which had for its object the presentation in France of songs from all countries. Lenormand did not set out in his book to

iii

propound a theory or give a dissertation on French impressionistic harmony. His purpose was in the main a practical one. It was to show the student-composer by a number of typical passages the various new devices and' treatments of chords as employed by his French contemporaries. His book is a sort of *catalogue raisonné* which, if it does not give the underlying idea of all the harmonic phenomena of his time, has the advantage of marshalling them in a comprehensive order. It goes without saying that the views expressed in this book necessarily differ from our present-day notions. After all what seemed so new and revolutionary at the beginning of our century has in the light of later experiences become a matter of course, and lost its appeal of novelty. This, however, does not in the least detract from the value of Lenormand's study, in which perhaps an additional interest will be found by comparing his views with our ideas on the subject. This, incidentally, was the main reason for republishing the book in its original, unaltered form.

Important as the harmonic writing of the French impressionists is, it represents only a part of the evolution of modern harmony. The writer of this preface has, therefore, issued, at the request of the publishers a sequel to the book dealing with the general development of Contemporary Harmony in other countries from 1914 onwards. It is thus hoped to give the student-composer a comprehensive survey of all the various devices which have combined to make twentieth-century harmony such a complicated and fascinating study.

MOSCO CARNER.

London,
June, 1940.

PREFACE

As human sensibility modifies itself ceaselessly during the course of the centuries, Music, its faithful interpreter, evolves side by side with it.*

A deep study of the continual transformations of the musical art would be out of place in this work, which is of an essentially modern character. We leave on one side the music of the Ancient Greeks, and also that of the Middle Ages, and consider only the great evolution of the seventeenth century.** This laid the foundations of the musical theory still used in our own days, and in its results, is of the highest importance. It was this that made possible the brilliant achievements of the 18th and 19th centuries.

Whether they wish it or not, all those who think musically are more or less impregnated with the idioms of that phase of the art.

But the page on which are inscribed the illustrious names of Bach, Mozart, Beethoven, Schumann, Wagner, etc., has scarcely been turned, when already new formulas appear.

The result of this state of things is that young musicians learn the practice of their art following the rules of the older technique, and then find themselves out of their bearings when they would write in the modern style; from which it arises that they fall into exaggerations for lack of the instruction appropriate to contemporary musical thought.

"But," say the theorists, "the teaching which we hold rests on immutable bases." This assertion is disputable. Is it not a little dangerous to speak of the immutability of a

---

* In our days this evolution proceeds so rapidly that a composer, arrived at the close of his career, has the sadness of being no longer in communion of idea with the young composers, unless he has kept his mind open to the constant transformation of the art. It is a curious fact that the majority of the elder musicians take sides against the new forms. Sincere and true artists — they are that, surely — should, it would seem, take a passionate interest in the evolution of the art. But these conclude, doubtless, that their works mark a definite, irrevocable condition.

** Evolution commencing from the 16th century.

system which relies on an artificial scale? At the present time this system consists of thirty-one sounds comprised within the compass of an octave. As a matter of fact these thirty-one sounds are reduced to twelve by the convention of *temperament*.*

---

* Although the system of temperament may be known to all, we think it may be useful to recall it. If, starting from a G♭♭, a series of rigorously exact ascending 5ths is built up, the 31 actual sounds which constitute our system will be obtained. The whole of the "Traité d'harmonie" of Gevaert (published by Lemoine) is based on that series of fifths. Whatever may be the note taken as the point of departure, at the twelfth successive fifth it will be perceived that the sounds no longer agree with the octave; so that in bringing these 31 sounds within the compass of the octave none is the equisonant of the other (see Fig. I). There has thus been made a compromise or mean in order to have but twelve sounds to the octave (Fig. II). This convention, which was made scientifically about 1700, has been called *tuning by equal temperament*. Guido d'Arezzo must have practised temperament, but it was not until later that Mersennus and afterwards Loulié and Sauveur put forward some scientific explanations. Rameau brought these to a more perfect development about 1720 in order afterwards to devote himself to the study of harmonics (Fig. III).

Fig. I. Theoretical system. (31 sounds.)			Fig. II. Practical system. (12 sounds.)		Fig. III. Natural sounds. (First harmonics.)
A×	B		B		
A♯		C♭	A♯ B♭		
		B♭	A		
G×	A	B♭♭	G♯ A♭		
G♯			G		
F×	G	A♭	F♯ G♭		
F♯		A♭♭	F		
E♯	F	G♭	E		
		G♭♭	D♯ E♭		
D×	E	F♭	D		
D♯		E♭	C♯ D♭		
C×	D	E♭♭	C		
C♯		D♭			
B♯	C	D♭♭			

In other words, we write music as if we had thirty-one sounds at our disposal, and we execute it by means of twelve sounds.

At the present time composers content themselves with a rejuvenation of the classical theory. It may be a day will come when they will weary of the false combination in which conception and execution are different one from the other.* But then, on which side will they find themselves?

Continuing to accept the thirty-one sounds and repudiating the *temperament,* will they demand untempered instruments? That would be logical, but it would revolutionise the manufacture of instruments.

In the above table (Fig. I) we represent the relative pitch of the different sounds according to the feeling of musicians, but while these maintain that C♯, for example, is higher than D♭, the physicists affirm the contrary. This contradiction may perhaps be explained if we admit that the semitone resulting from the calculation of the physicists has not the same origin as that of the musicians.

In the bulletin No. 2 (1908) of the Institut Psychologique, M. Jean Marnold has made an interesting communication as to the possibility of bringing the musician and the physicist into agreement. Incidentally he reproaches composers for their ignorance in the matter of acoustics. Perhaps they are wrong in taking too little interest in this question; but what can they do, if it is not to be connected with *temperament,* while waiting for the theorists to understand each other sufficiently to give them a logical system *in which theory and practice shall be in agreement?*

* Musicians who play instruments with variable sounds justify themselves by saying: "We do not play the tempered notes; we play the music as it is written." This is perhaps true of the string quartet, or any other groups not comprising instruments with fixed sounds, but it is very highly contestable whenever the two kinds are used in combination. An orchestra, when it accompanies a concerto for the piano — an instrument with fixed sounds — is compelled to play tempered sounds if it does not wish to play out of tune.

Besides, an orchestra comprises some instruments of fixed sounds; if some artists were to play the Pythagorean sounds, as they claim, the others playing the tempered sounds, the effect would be very disagreeable; while if a third class of instrumentalists played the natural sounds it would result in incredible discord. The imperfection of the auditory organ of some would, perhaps, enable them to bear it, but reason could not allow it. And as for Chamber music with the piano; would composers and virtuosos who have passed their lives composing and playing music for piano and string instruments really have borne this continual dissonance, if it had been actually produced? And Vocal music! In his "Principes du Système musical et de l'Harmonie" (J. Hamelle), M. Anselme Vinée says: "Contrary to a common opinion it is physiologically impossible for the voice, accompanied by an instrument of unchangeable sounds, to emit tempered intervals. When its natural intonation leads to a sound in discord with the note fixed at the moment, a union must quickly be produced, but always by flexion." Without entering into the learned considerations of M. Vinée (see his treatise, pp. 41 and 64), it suffices in the present case that we state the fact of this union.

Will they shape their thought to the scale of natural sounds, with its harmonics not included in the present system? The attempt has just been made.*

Will they adopt, in theory, the division of the octave into twelve equal semitones, as it in practice exists for instruments with fixed sounds? That would not change the sound of the music, but would modify the theory and banish the accidental signs ♯, ♭ and ♮.** This would be the end of the system of thirty-one sounds, and also of *temperament.*

In any case, it is impossible that theoretical music and practical music will not end by coming into agreement with each other. One can foresee that this will not be done without severe struggles. "The time has not yet arrived" say the professors; "one must learn one's trade well with the

---

For us, although the voice and the instruments with variable sounds can execute the thirty-one sounds of our theoretical system, it seems proved that as soon as an instrument of fixed sounds is heard simultaneously with them, all artists, instinctively, sing and play the tempered note :—that is, as we have said before, interpret through the medium of twelve notes that which is written for thirty-one notes. That statement, carefully checked, would be of great importance to the partisans of the theoretical division of the scale into twelve equal spaces.

* The Russian composer, Scriabine, in his "Prometheus" for orchestra, has just written the novel scale
C, D, E, F♯, A, B♭.
formed of the 8th, 9th, 10th, 11th, 13th and 14th harmonics (see Fig. 3, page vi); the orchestra does not play the tempered sounds, it plays the natural sounds by taking count of the actual pitch of numbers 11, 13, and 14. "Musique à Moscou"; Nicolas Petroff; *Monde Musical;* 30th June 1911.

** In the "Cours de Composition Musicale," of M. Vincent d'Indy (Vol. I, 1902, Durand), his collaborator, M. Auguste Sèrieyx, gives in a note (p. 62) some personal ideas on the suppression of the accidental signs (♯, ♭, ♮), by the employment of a staff of which each degree (line or space) represents invariably a tempered semitone.

More recently, M. Menchaca, an Argentine theorist, has brought forward a system of notation, which we cannot explain here, but the result of which is the division of the octave into twelve equal intervals.

The names chosen by M. Menchaca for his scale of twelve degrees are: do, dou, re, ro, mi, fa, fe, sol, nou, la, se, si. Some of these may be replaced with advantage, for they seem to suggest a certain relation between the notes, which, under these conditions ought not to exist. This theorist himself makes the observation that a certain number of vibrations produces a fixed sound, and that there is no reason for connecting that sound with its neighbours. "Each sound is or is not; it has a physical existence which cannot be modified." "Système Musical Menchaca" (Pleyel, Lyon & Co.). The scale of twelve degrees suppresses the accidental signs: "The ♯ and the ♭ are of all known musical characters the most vexatiously conventional."

The first difficulty to be overcome, if a change of system is to be arrived at, will be to find a mode of notation for this scale of twelve degrees — that of M. Menchaca would appear to be difficult of application to polyphonic music. The problem does not appear to be insoluble, and we know that on many sides attempts are being made to solve it.

present system." Without doubt, but it is to be wished that it should be done under such conditions that once the studies are completed the creative faculty shall not be forced into a groove.*

In matters of art it is dangerous to learn to do as others do. Certainly it is necessary to consult tradition in order to interpret the masterpieces of the past; but to invoke tradition when it is a question of creating — is not that a false way which can only lead to a plagiarising of one's predecessors?

To return to Modern Harmony: that which makes the new school particularly interesting is the considerable effort it is making to free itself from the laws of the older technique without having any other guide save the intuition of a new idea of beauty. Certain authors — and this is a widespread idea in the world of amateurs — imagine that in these days one can write "no matter what." They misunderstand the character of the evolution of to-day. The most daring composers are all technicians of the greatest ability.** Those who unite to such mastery the greater gift of a truly musical temperament bring themselves naturally to the first rank. The others, complicating the harmony simply with the pleasure of the grammarian, class themselves rather among the theorists than among the creators, which nevertheless assures them an important place.

The harmony called *modern*, considered as a means of technique does not suffice to constitute *a modern music*. Such compositions, where are to be found gathered together all the new devices, often give only a negative impression. On the other hand, some works based on harmonies relatively simple can invoke an intensely modern atmosphere.*** Above the manner of writing there is, therefore, *the modern inspiration*, and the musicians of classical education make a mistake when they complicate their harmonies thinking

---

* A composer very much to the front, who belongs to the modern school, declares that he himself has found several years of desperate effort necessary to get rid of the impressions received in the time of his studentship, and to re-establish his individuality.

** We speak of serious and well-instructed artists, leaving on one side the crowd of imitators, with whom the search after strange and weird harmonies only serves to hide their ignorance and absolute lack of musicality.

*** There are to be found many examples in the music of M. Gabriel Fauré, who, by the peculiar and charming turn he gives to some harmonic combinations, which are relatively little complicated, is one of the most modern composers of our epoch. The precursor of the movement of to-day, with which he still remains associated by his productions, his position in the history of French music will be important.

thus to modernise themselves. Before all else they must write with the sincerity of their inspiration and of their feeling.

The composers who, about forty years ago, contributed to the evolution of the art with all the ardour of their youth, fulfilled their duty at a useful time. Present-day masters maintain an obstinate struggle for the acceptance of the new formulas which are imposed on them by the inevitable transformation of all things — an irresistible force to which they are compelled to submit. One may overwhelm them by comparing their works with those of the masters of the past; but the question is not one of knowing whether they are doing better or worse than their predecessors. Their mission as composers, that is, *inventors*, of music, is to manifest their sensibility in a new language, to write something other than that which has already been written.

The new school* makes itself known by works of a peculiar charm, which are not without some affinity with other more pretentious and unmusical productions. Must there be seen in these only a refinement of the older art, or are they to be considered as the beginning of a new art? It is difficult to foresee the answer which our descendants will make to these two questions.** As to those who imagine that a return will be made to the past, or who think that a new genius will be brought to light through the medium of the technique and æsthetic of the past, their illusion, we believe, is complete. There can no more be a new Beethoven than there can be a new Christopher Columbus.

While waiting for the didactic work which will build up, it may be, a new musical system, it has seemed to us interesting to extract some of the most typical harmonic examples that we have met with in the works of modern authors. We must ask the young harmonist who may read this little book to consider it as a document of transition between the treatises of the past and those of the future, as a sort of inventory of modern harmony; as a landmark planted in a vast field of sonorous vibrations which musicians have been indefatigably clearing for more than twenty-five centuries.

RENÉ LENORMAND.***

---

* By the audacity of his harmonies and also by their charm and musicality, M. Debussy may be considered as the chief of this school. Doubtless he had his precursors, he has his emulators, he will have his successors; but the score of "Pelleas et Melisande" marks an epoch in the history of the art.

** See Chap. XII. Conclusions.

*** I owe an explanation to those of my friends who may be surprised at the tendencies of this publication. I am going to give it them, and in so doing must apologise for speaking of myself. It is absurd to suppose that musical evolution can stand still at any moment whatever of its history; and there is no reason for a composer, whatever may be his age, or whatever his production, to show himself indifferent or hostile to that evolution. But neither that which is nor that which shall be can destroy that which has been. I have therefore been able to write this little work without abandoning anything of my profound admiration for the Masters of the past, and without abjuring any of my productions which, good or bad, remain the sincere expression of a feeling which time has been able to modify.

R. L.

EXPLANATORY NOTES

In order not to multiply beyond measure the number of our quotations, we had intended to confine our choice to the most typical examples met with in works themselves considered as typical. On consideration, we have adopted the plan of consulting a large number of works in order to evoke more completely the "atmosphere" in which the modern French school lives and moves.

Here in alphabetical order is a list of composers whose works are quoted:

MM. Louis Aubert, Alfred Bruneau, Caplet, E. Chabrier, E. Chausson, Claude Debussy, Paul Dukas, Gabriel Dupont, Fanelli, Gabriel Fauré, Alexandre Georges, Jean Huré, Vincent d'Indy, Charles Koechlin, René Lenormand, Ernest Moret, Léon Moreau, Maurice Ravel, Albert Roussel, Samuel Rousseau, Saint-Saëns, Erik Satie, Florent Schmitt, Déodat de Sévérac and Woollett.

As will be seen by this list, this little book is almost exclusively French in its scope.

It goes without saying that we are concerned only with harmonic facts, or with modes of writing which present a modern feeling.

We have no intention of proposing a new system or of writing a treatise on harmony; we present merely a collection of examples which we have explained as far as possible through the medium of the earlier technique.*

---

* In order to reckon with some of the processes of the modern school it will be well to refer to the harmonic series:

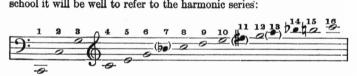

Here will be found, we believe, the origin of a certain number of progressions reproved by classical teaching.

Some of the authors quoted have willingly helped us to make a *précis* of their intentions, and to them we present our sincere thanks. If in these notes the celebrated names of MM. Massenet, Dubois, etc., etc., are not met with, it is that these masters, of an indisputable talent, have doubtless judged that the harmonic innovations with which we

---

In no case must any too definite statements be based on the harmonic series, because, not only do the sounds 7, 11 and 13 lack preciseness, but the whole series may be found to be modified by the manner in which the sounding body is set in vibration.

The harmonic series has been requisitioned in all possible fashions; from it have been deduced a number of systems more or less ingenious, more or less erroneous. We will add nothing to these labours of physicists who surpass us in competence, but limit ourselves to a simple deduction which is to be found formulated in Chapter II and also, partially, in Chapter I.

It may not be useless, and in any case it will be interesting, to run through the different systems that sprang up after Rameau. Here are the names of the authors of *some* of these treatises: — Marpurg, Testori, the Abbé Roussier, Levens, Sorge, Père Valloti, Père Sabbatini, the Abbé Vogler, Knecht, Daube, Schroeter, Kirnberger, Gottfried Weber, Derode, Langlé, Reicha, Berton, Catel, de Momigny, Blein, Schneider, Jelensperger, Fétis, etc., etc. We stop this list about the middle of the 19th century, at which period appeared the treatises known to all. The name of Rameau dominates this enormous effort; his theories were the origin of all these frequently contradictory systems, and remained in use until the coming of Catel.

And looking over these older works several interesting names are encountered: —Père Sabbatini among others, who after having worked with Père Martini placed himself under the direction of Père Valotti, Maestro di Cappella at St. Anthony's, Padua. Valotti published only the first part of his treatise (*Della Scienza Teorica e practica della Moderna Musica*, libro primo, in Padova 1779) and it was Sabbatini who formulated the harmonies of his master. They did not fail of a certain modern savour as may be judged by the following: —

To the common chord he added the 9th and presented it thus:

We may notice that the common chord with the 9th added — it is not a chord of the 9th — is often to be met with in the modern school (Chap. IV [9]). It may be analysed as an appoggiatura sounded against the harmony-note.

To the common chord he added also the 11th, which may be analysed like the preceding: i.e., as an appoggiatura sounded at the same time as the harmony-note.

are concerned, were contrary to their æsthetic principles, and, save with rare exceptions, they have not employed them.

Père Sabbatini — coming at least two centuries too soon — stated that the inversion of a 9th was a 7th.   So, the modern school frequently employs the 9th below the root in inversions of chords of the 9th (Chap. III [14]).   They use even the 4th inversion of the chord of the 9th, pronounced impracticable by the classical theorists.   (Chap. III [11] Chap. XI [19]).

CHAPTER I

TWO OR MORE CONSECUTIVE FIFTHS

By Similar and Conjunct Motion

These are forbidden, say the treatises of harmony in use to-day. They do not explain why a composer should not write two or more consecutive fifths in similar and conjunct motion, if these fifths correspond with a musical intention which cannot be realised without their occurrence.

It seems that the feeling of repose evoked by that interval, which requires nothing after it, must secure it against any very free movement. Without attaching too much importance to the fact, it is not without use to remember that the 5th is the 3rd of the harmonic series. Thus, a somewhat refined ear can distinguish quite clearly the 3rd harmonic; consequently each time that a composer sounds two notes on conjunct degrees, he sounds at the same time two consecutive fifths by similar and conjunct motion:

This is an "indication" that is not without value, relative to the possibility of using fifths with the bass. There should be no confusion of the natural harmonic of which we speak with the artificial harmonics of the mutation stops of the organ.

* * *

Besides, fifths have always been written:

Melody in the Dorian mode — ancient Greek — accompanied by the upper fifth: *Traité d'harmonie* by Gevaert (Lemoine, publisher).

1

In the middle ages all the chants and melodies were accompanied at the fifth or at the fourth; the different combinations which they formed were designated by the general name of *Organum*. On this subject Hucbald wrote with enthusiasm: "You will see a suave harmony born of this combination."*

Organum
at the 5th

Nos qui vi-vi-mus be -ne- di- ci- mus Do- mi-num

Organum
at the 4th
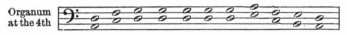

Tu pa - tris sem - pi - ter -nus es fi - li - us

Little by little consecutive fifths were abandoned, and at the commencement of the 14th century we find them forbidden by Jean de Muris. We must say that Gevaert has attributed their first prohibition to Tinctoris in the 15th century. Nevertheless, Jean de Muris is very explicit with regard to successive fifths.

* * *

The masters of the period which immediately preceded our own have carefully avoided them. Nevertheless, there are few authors in whose works some are not to be met with.

---

* *Histoire de la Musique Moderne*, Marcillac (Fischbacher).

** Kiesewetter has disputed the practical existence of Organum, seeing in it only an aberration of the theorist. *Geschichte der europæisch-abendliechen or unsrer heutigen Musik*, 2nd ed. (Leipsic). From all the evidence it appears that he was mistaken, and that successions of fifths were in use in the Middle Ages.

In the country churches, when the faithful sing in unison, it often happens that some among them accompany the women's voices a 4th below and the men's voices a 5th above; that is the old *Organum*. M. Lavignac has noticed, as we have, and has justly remarked (*La Musique et les Musiciens*, Delagrave), that the fifth and the fourth are the intervals which most resemble the octave: octave ⅔, fifth ⅔, fourth ¾.

It is probable that these peasants, lacking musical education, imagined themselves singing at the octave or unison with the other voices.

We may quote the following examples:

ROSSINI. *William Tell.* (2nd Act.)

BEETHOVEN. *Eroica Symphony.* (1st movement.)

It is interesting to note the care that Beethoven has taken to allow the recollection of each fifth to be lost before attacking another.

SCHUMANN, Op. 26. *Finale.*

Here are some fragments of modern works.   The successions of fifths here are used under the conditions which are summarised at the end of the chapter.

CLAUDE DEBUSSY.   *Chansons de Bilitis.*   (Fromont, Pubr.)

(1) *Lento:* The 5th doubled, proceeds by contrary motion.
(2) *Lento:* Several consecutive fifths by disjunct motion.

Study of Modern Harmony.

(3)   (4)   (5)   (6)   See the "Deductions" page 11.

CH. KOECHLIN.   *Les rêves morts.*   Op. 13, No. 2.
L'astre rouge.   Op. 13.   (Rouart & Lerolle, Pubr.)

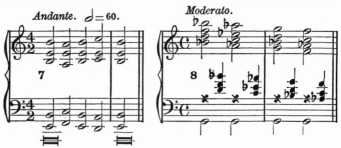

(7) Fifths between the inner parts, with contrary motion of the upper part.
(8) Fifths between the inner parts.

ALEXANDRE GEORGES. *Hymne au soleil.* (Enoch, Pubr.)

Je   t'of - fre   cet   or   vi -

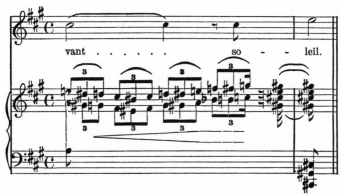

vant . . . . . .   so - - leil.

(9) Chromatic fifths.

SAMUEL ROUSSEAU. *La Cloche du Rhin* (1898). Page 11.

(Choudens, Pubr.)

(10) Fifths by Chromatic steps; the 3rd is common to the two chords.

G. FAURÉ. *Le Secret.*   *Prison.* (J. Hamelle, Pubr.)

(11) Fifths with similar motion in all the parts.
(12) Fifths between the outer parts with similar motion in all the parts.

SAINT–SAËNS. *5th Pianoforte Concerto.* (Durand, Pubr.)

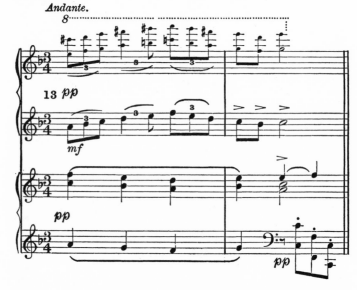

(13) In performance the listener cannot but notice an imitation of percussion instruments used in the East.   Organists who have taken part in performances of the Oratorios and Cantatas of Handel and Bach, under the direction of Gevaert, know that erudite musician forbade the use of mutation stops, finding that the artificial harmonics conflicted with the natural harmonics of the Orchestra.   The use which M. Saint-Saëns makes of them on the piano (sounds 3 & 5) is both original and piquant.

DÉODAT de SÉVERAC.   *Un rêve.*   (Edition mutuelle.)

(14) Fifths between the lower parts, with oblique motion of an inner‑part.

RENÉ LENORMAND.   *Pièces exotiques.*   (J. Hamelle, Pubr.)

(15) Fifths caused by the melodic outline; contained within the limits of the octave.

E. MORET.   *Préludes,* (*No. 9*).   (Heugel, Pubr.)

(16) Chord of the 6th and 3rd arranged so that the 3rd is above the 6th, which causes the fifth between the two upper parts.

E. MORET.   *Interlude.   Impression de neige.*   (Heugel, Pubr.)

(17) Continued in the same manner for several bars.   The fifths here do not result from the progression of the parts in the harmonic tissue.   It is a melody accompanied by the fifth continuously.   The sound of the same interval indefinitely repeated causes monotony.   In the present case, *Impression de neige,* the effect is intended by the author, and the fifths evoke effectively the sombre melancholy of a snowy day.

CLAUDE DEBUSSY.   *Hommage à Rameau.*   (Durand, (Pubr.)

(18) etc.   See the Deductions, page 11, No. 3.

RENÉ LENORMAND. *Le voyage imaginaire — Chapelle bretonne,*
(1889). (J. Hamelle, Pubr.)

(19) Fifths between the lower parts.

H. WOOLLETT. *La neige.* (Hamelle, Pubr.)

(20) Fifths in two octaves, with similar motion in all parts.

ALEXANDRE GEORGES. *Miarka.* Page 255. (Enoch, Pubr.)

(21) Fifths by semitones
between the outer parts.

A. BRUNEAU. *Le Rêve* (1891). (Choudens, Pubr.)

page 2.

(22) Fifths by disjunct motion, with notes in common between the
chords.

page 9.

(23) Fifths with the bass, duplicated in other parts.

SAINT–SAËNS.   *Le Pas d'Armes du Roi Jean.*   (Durand, Pubr.)
     Animato.

(24) This work was composed in 1852 (when the composer was 17 years of age) and published in 1855.   The fifths are intended to give an impression of bells.

DEDUCTIONS

Without any intention of formulating new rules, we may, by generalising from the foregoing instances, deduce the following indications having special relation to the modern style.

(1). Two or more fifths in succession, in similar and conjunct motion, are readily used in the two lowest parts,* where the upper parts proceed by contrary or oblique motion. (1), (10), (14).

(2). They are also used in the two lowest parts, accompanied by similar motion in all the parts. These successions of fifths are generally short, and will be so much the better if some precautions are taken as to the mode of approaching and leaving them, e.g. : —

(i.) The last fifth approached by disjunct motion with a note in common between the chords. (3), (5).

(ii.) The fifths proceeding by similar and conjunct motion, the last fifth accompanied by some contrary motion in the upper part. (4), (6).

(iii.) Successions of fifths which terminate by similar motion are met with; but they are more rarely found.

(3). Used in the upper parts they may be presented in two ways: —

(i.) Bare fifths (16), (17). They are thus very prominent, and a number cannot be heard in succession without monotony. In alternation with other intervals that effect is modified. (11), (15).

---

* Classical teaching admits the possibility of certain fifths by semi-tone.

TH. DUBOIS. *Notes et études d'harmonie.* Page 97. (Heugel, Pubr.)

("Tolerable, even for the student, by placing them in the lowest parts.") (Th. Dubois).

This work completes the "Traité de Reber," and one or other may always be consulted for everything which relates to classical technique.

(ii.) If the third is added, a succession of chords of three
notes in root position is given; the adding of the
lower octave of the fifth gives a chord of a disposition specially suited to the pianoforte, and of
great sonority. (18).

(4). Fifths are of good effect in the inner parts, particularly when they are associated with contrary motion in the
other parts. (7) If they result from chords of the 6th and
3rd with the parts doubled (a combination practised for
many years), they lose some of their character. (8).

(5). They are more rarely used between the extreme parts
by similar motion in all the parts. (12), (21).

(6). By disjunct motion they are readily used with notes
in common between the chords. (2), (22).

(7). Chromatic fifths may be freely used. (9), (21).

(8). If a long succession of fifths is given in the lower
parts, they cease to form a part of the harmonic tissue.
(19), (20), (23).

(9). They may always be used where the composer has
a definite aim (13), (15), (22); but they are still forbidden
whenever they are the result of awkwardness or lack of
skill in writing; a prohibition, moreover, which may be
applied to any interval whatever.

CHAPTER II

CHORDS OF THE SEVENTH

One knows that by resolving a chord of the seventh on a chord a fifth below, what is called the natural resolution is obtained. Under the name of exceptional resolutions many others are used, either by retaining the seventh, or by making it rise or fall by conjunct degrees, and proceeding to any other chord but that of a fifth below. We find the "recipe" for these resolutions in all treatises on Harmony.

The modern school has further enlarged the circle of these resolutions by making chords of the seventh move by similar and conjunct motion in all parts, ascending or descending. We may add that, usual or exceptional, these resolutions may be made by interchange of parts. As we shall see, all modern authors write these successions.*

---

* These resolutions may find their origin, if not their justification, in the succession of two notes by conjunct motion. Taking for example, the sound of C; we have the first harmonics as follows:

Thus, a practised ear will distinguish the odd harmonics, 3, 5 and 7, as those which give the following chord of the 7th

making some reservation as to the just intonation of the sound No. 7.

If after the note C, we sound that of D, it produces a new series of harmonics:

EXAMPLES

G. FAURÉ. *Le parfum impérissable.*   (J. Hamelle, Pubr.)

(1) Succession by conjunct motion, descending, of two third-inversions of the chord of the 7.*

---

* The small + always indicates the presence of the leading note. (Translator.)

This gives us a new chord of the 7th (with the same reservation for the sound No. 7).

The D coming immediately after the C, the first chord is succeeded by the second by similar and conjunct motion in all the parts:

Modern composers may, therefore, allege that they do nothing but work in the mould which Nature indicates to them. It is an indication that is not easily seen, it is true, but of which, nevertheless, account may be taken.

If, continuing to accept the sound 7 as a minor 7th, the harmonic ninth is added, a succession of chords of the 9th will be obtained by conjunct degrees:

E. CHAUSSON. *Serres chaudes.* Page 6. (Rouart et Lerolle, Pubr.)

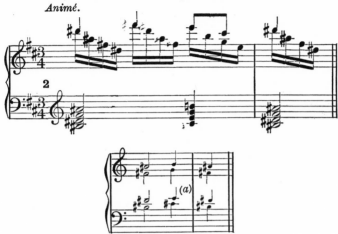

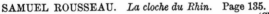

(2) Chords of the 7th by conjunct motion. They may also be analysed as, (*a*) ornamentation of the 3rd, 5th and 7th, the succession of two chords of the 7th, however, remaining.

SAMUEL ROUSSEAU. *La cloche du Rhin.* Page 135.

(Choudens, Pubr.)

It may be objected that if several notes are heard simultaneously, they produce so many series of harmonics that the mixture reduces the importance of the above deductions. That is true, and therefore, we give them only as a theoretical suggestion.

(3) (*a*) (*b*) Chords of the 7th by conjunct degrees. (*b*) E is an appoggiatura. (*c*) Change of the chord on the resolution of the appoggiatura. (E♯ for F.)

Andantino.   page 201.

(4) Second inversions of the chord of ₇ moving by conjunct degrees and similar motion in all the parts.

page 138.

(5) Successions of second inversions of chords of the 7th by conjunct and similar motion in all the parts. The presence of the 9th in the upper part does not alter the character of the succession.

page 59. *8va*..

Passing chords.

page 88.

(7) Succession of chords of the 7th of the 3rd species* by semitones and similar movement in all the parts under an inverted pedal.

page 68.   (c)

(8) (a) Chords of the 7th by conjunct degrees.
     (b) Resolution by interchange of parts.
     (c) Alteration of the 5th.

A. BRUNEAU. *Messidor.* Page 211.   (Choudens, Pubr.)

(9) Succession of chords of the 7th by conjunct degrees, (b) becoming the chord of the 9th at (c).

We may also say that this is a chord of E minor succeeded by the chord of the 9th on G, with passing notes in the bass; but the pause on C♯ gives it the character of a chord of the seventh, and, when it is followed by the chord of the seventh on B, two chords of the seventh are heard by conjunct motion.

---

* (Translator's note: This method of numbering the Species of Chords will be explained by reference to example (22) in this Chapter.)

G. FAURÉ. *Le parfum impérissable.*   (J. Hamelle, Pubr.)

Andante.

(10) Resolution by interchange of parts.

(10²) A peculiar charm resulting from the very free movement of the parts.

G. FAURÉ. *Adieu.*   (Durand, Pubr.)

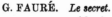

(11) Resolution by interchange of parts.

G. FAURÉ. *Le secret.*   *Au cimetière.*   (J. Hamelle, Pubr.)

Adagio.   *Andante.*

(12) Resolution by interchange of parts.
(12²) Resolution by interchange of parts.

E. CHABRIER. *Le roi malgré lui.* (Enoch, Pubr.)
page 52.

(13) 1st inversions of the chords of the 7th, moving by step.

LÉON MOREAU. *Dans la nuit.* (Pfister, Pubr.)

(14) Successions of the second inversion of chords of the seventh.

Study of Modern Harmony.
Allegro.

(15) Chord of the 7th of the 4th species mixed with the other species.

Study of Modern Harmony.

(16) Chords of the 7th of the first species by similar and conjunct motion in all the parts.* There are to be found in Chopin and Schumann some successions of chords of the 7th moving by step.

CHABRIER. *Briséis.* Page 28.   (Enoch, Pubr.)

(17) Successions of the first inversion of chords of the 7th of the first species.

---

* It will be useful to recall here the close of the 21st Mazurka of Chopin; —

CLAUDE DEBUSSY. *Pelléas et Mélisande.* (Durand, Pubr.)

Et voi - ci des traces de sang.

page 5.

(18) Successions of the 3rd inversion of the chord of the 7th of the 1st species with altered 5th.

page 84.

Oh ! . . . ces pe-ti-tes mains.

(19) Succession of the 4th inversion of chords of the 7th by conjunct degrees (see previous note).

and also this bar of Schumann, *Scherzino* Op. 26, No. 3.

(20) Successions of 3rd inversions of various kinds on a pedal.

CLAUDE DEBUSSY. *Pelléas et Mélisande.* Durand, Pubr.)

(21) Successions of chords of the 7th of the 3rd species by conjunct degrees.

page 114.

3rd. 2nd. 1st. 4th.

(22) Successions of inversions of the four species of chords of the 7th.

page 10. *Animé.*

(23) Chord of the 7th with the 6th replacing the 5th.

The minor 6th having the same sound as the augmented 5th we can analyse the chord as a chord of the 7 with augmented 5th. This example finds a place here only for the purpose of showing the cause of No. 6 of·the Deductions.

A. BRUNEAU. *Messidor.* Page 280. (Choudens, Pubr.)

(24) Succession of two chords of the 7th by conjunct motion of the bass and of the 7th, but with two notes in common; we mention this because of the movement of the two sevenths.

M. RAVEL.   *Sur l'herbe.*   (Durand, Pubr.)

Cevin de Chypre est exquis
très expressif.

(25)   (a) Inversions of the chords of the 7th moving by semitones.
        (b) Passing note.
        (c) G is an appoggiatura.
        (d) Pedal.

G. FAURÉ.   *La bonne Chanson.*   No. 5.   (J. Hamelle, Pubr.)

CLAUDE DEBUSSY.   *Pelléas et Mélisande.*   Page 26.   (Durand, Pubr.)

(27) Chords of the 7th of the 1st species, moving by conjunct and similar motion, with an inverted pedal, which note is an integral part of all the chords.

CLAUDE DEBUSSY. *Pelléas et Mélisande.* Page 204. (Durand, Pubr.)

(28) Succession of chords of the 7th of the 3rd species, moving by step.

DEDUCTIONS

We cannot repeat too often that we have no intention of formulating the rules of a new technique. In saying that modern composers use successions of chords of the seventh under the following conditions, we limit ourselves to observed facts.

(1). Two or more chords of the seventh of the first species may proceed by step (either of a tone or a semitone) and by similar motion in all the parts, ascending or descending, either in root position or in their inversions. (1), (3), (5), (13), (14), (16), (17), (26), (27).

(2). Chords of the seventh of the second species, whilst they may proceed under the same conditions as those of the first species, do not give so satisfying an impression. The more they are associated with other species the better they sound. (15), (19), (22), (24).

(3). Chords of the seventh of the third species are used under the same conditions as chords of the diminished seventh. (2), (6), (7), (9), (21), (28).

(4). The first inversion of the chord of the seventh of the fourth species lends itself better than other positions of that chord to successions by conjunct and similar motion — particularly by step of a semitone. Nevertheless, mixed with other species, it is used, as they are, in the root position as well as inverted. (15), (19), (22).

(5). In all the foregoing successions it must be noticed that the disposition of the parts plays an important *rôle*. In the inversions, the interval of the seventh is preferred to that of the second, although that arrangement may be practicable. (13), (25).

(6). Chords of the seventh with an augmentation of the fifth may proceed, in descending, by similar and conjunct motion. (18).

As the augmented fifth is the enharmonic of the minor sixth, these intervals are often written interchangeably. (23).

(7). Resolutions by interchange of parts are readily used. It suffices that the note of resolution be heard in any one of the parts whatsoever. (10), (11), (12).

CHAPTER III

CHORDS OF THE NINTH*

Chords of the ninth have, like chords of the seventh, their natural resolutions and those called exceptional. Both are found in all treatises on harmony, and have been exploited by all composers. We will concern ourselves now only with the resolutions which belong to the modern school, viz.: the succession of two chords of the ninth moving by step and in similar motion in all the parts.** We will add to these several resolutions little used in the classical technique.

The resolution of the ninth upon another such ninth by conjunct movement offends the sensibilities of many musicians; it is certain that two bare ninths in succession are unpleasant; but they are not at all disagreeable, and the ear accepts them readily, if the complete chord of the ninth is used, as it occurs in the harmonic series:

In all the successions which follow, the disposition of the parts is very important.

---

* The French treatises of Reber-Dubois and of Durand recognise but one chord of the ninth (major or minor). M. Gevaert in his "Traité d'harmonie" (Lemoine, Publisher), has admitted four species:

Chords of the 9th of 1st Species		Chords of the 9th of 2nd Species		Chords of the 9th of the 3rd Species.	Chords of the 9th of the 4th species.
with major ninth.	with minor ninth.	with major ninth.	with minor ninth.		

** See Chapter II, Chords of the Seventh, notes on the harmonic series.

EXAMPLES

G. FAURÉ.   *Prison.*   (J. Hamelle, Pubr., 1891.)
Quasi adagio.

(1) Succession of two chords of the major 9th of the first species, moving by the descent of a major 2nd.

G. FAURÉ.   *La bonne Chanson.*   (J. Hamelle, Pubr.)
Allegretto con moto.

(2) (*a*) Succession of two chords of the minor 9th of the first species, the first moving to the second by the descent of a minor 3rd, merely by change of root.

CLAUDE DEBUSSY.   *Children's Corner.*   (Durand, Pubr.)

(3) Chords of the 9th proceeding by minor thirds upwards.

CLAUDE DEBUSSY. *Chansons de Bilitis.* (Fromont, Pubr.)

(4) Successions of chords of the 9th of the 1st and 2nd species.

CLAUDE DEBUSSY. *Chansons de Bilitis.* (Fromont, Pubr.)

(5) Chords of the 9th proceeding by chromatic semitones.

CLAUDE DEBUSSY. *Chansons de Bilitis.* (Fromont, Pubr.)

(6) Common chords with appoggiaturas, or chords of the 9th with passing notes. Whichever interpretation be adopted, there is a succession of chords of the 9th proceeding by thirds upwards.

CLAUDE DEBUSSY. *Pelléas et Mélisande.*   Page 233.   (Durand, Pubr.)

(7) Chords of the 9th and the 7th alternately, by conjunct motion.
(*a*) 4th species.   (*b*) 2nd species.   (*c*) 4th species.

page 232.

(8) (*a*) Chords of the 9th proceeding by 3rds downwards.
     (*b*) Chords of the 9th proceeding by 3rds upwards.
     (*c*) Chords of the 9th proceeding by conjunct degrees.

page 80.

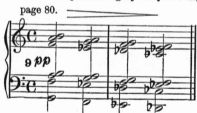

(9) Chords of the 9th by descending major seconds.

page 242.

(9)² Chords of the 9th by chromatic degrees.

FLORENT SCHMITT. *La Tragédie de Salomé.* (Jacques Durand, Pubr.)

Prélude. Lento.

(10) Inverted ninths (keys of B minor and A minor) on the un-raised 7th degree, with dominant pedal.

FLORENT SCHMITT. *La Tragédie de Salomé.* (Jacques Durand, Pubr.)

Danse de l'Effroi.

(11) 4th inversion of the chord of the dominant 9th (key of G major).

FLORENT SCHMITT. *Psalm XLVI.* (Mathot, Pubr.)

(12) 9th with major 7th (that is, the chord of the 9th of the 4th species).

FLORENT SCHMITT.   *Trois rapsodies.*   (Durand, Pubr.)

(13) (*a*) Ninth with double alteration and anticipation in the upper part.

(14) (*a*) and (*b*) Chords of the 9th of which the root and the 9th appear at the interval of a 7th from one another by the 9th being below the root.

FLORENT SCHMITT.   *Quintette pour piano et cordes.*   (Mathot, Pubr.)

(15) (*a*) Dominant 9th complete, with, added, alterations of the 5th and the 7th.

(16) Resolution of the 9th.

CH. KŒCHLIN. *Le sommeil de Canope.* (Rouart & Lerolle.)

(17) (*a*) D♯ and G♯ appoggiaturas.
      (*b*) 1st inversion of the chord of the dominant 9th, the root in the upper part and E an appoggiatura.
      (*c*) D♯ an unresolved appoggiatura in chord of + ᵒ.
      (*d*) Chord of + ⁶, with E an unresolved appoggiatura.
      (*e*) Chord of + ᵒ with F an appoggiatura.
      (*f*) 2nd inversion of chord of the 9th.

(*g*) 2nd inversion of chord of the dominant minor 9th with B♮ appoggiatura.
(*h*) 2nd inversion of chord of the diminished 7th with G appoggiatura.
(*i*) Chord of the dominant minor 9th; A♮ is an appoggiatura and B♮ a passing pedal-note of the tonic. (Sustained from previous chord. Translator).

CH. KŒCHLIN. *Chant de Kala Nag.* (Rouart & Lerolle, Pubr.)

(18) Chords of the 9th proceeding by step at (*a*) and by diminished 4th at (*b*) with a note in common. (F$\sharp$ = G$\flat$.)

Study of Modern Harmony.

(19) (*a*) 3rd inversions of the chord of the major 9th proceeding by step (whole tone).

(*b*) 3rd inversions of the chord of the 9th, major and minor, proceeding by step (semitone).

(20) Succession, by descending semitone, of 3rd inversions of chord of the minor 9th.

CH. KŒCHLIN. *Prélude.*

(21) Succession of 1st inversions of chords of the 9th by conjunct degrees.

E. CHABRIER. *Le roi malgré lui* (1887). (Enoch, Pubr.)
page 330.

E. CHABRIER. *Le roi malgré lui.* (Enoch, Pubr.)
page 229.

M. RAVEL. *Sur l'herbe.* (Durand, Pubr.)

(24) (*a*) The 9th against the root in the upper parts. The root takes
the character of a pedal in an inner part.

Although the foregoing explanation is the better one, it may also be considered that it is the G which forms the pedal.

M. RAVEL.   *L'heure espagnole.*   (Durand, Pubr.)

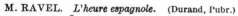

(*a*) Pedal on F♯.
(*b*) Chords of the minor 9th with altered 5th proceeding by semitones.

(*c*) Pedal in inner part on F♮, taken and quitted regularly on an integral note.   That makes a double pedal, F♯ — F♮.
(*d*) It is in the mind of the composer to consider the notation of the song of the birds as a picturesque, extra-musical effect.   Particularly is this so in that which concerns the first passage (Petit Coq), of which the notation is only approximate.   This sound, which perhaps approximates to that of percussion instruments, is produced by the reed of the double bassoon separated from the instrument.

M. RAVEL.   *Miroirs.*   (*Noctuelle*).   (Demets, Pubr.)

(26) Chords of the 9th by conjunct motion at (*a*), and by upward 3rd at (*b*), with appoggiatura and passing notes.

G. FAURE.   *Thême et Variations.*   (J. Hamelle, Pubr.)

(27) Resolutions of chords of the 7th and of the 9th by 5th downwards.

Study of Modern Harmony.

Combination of chords of the major and minor 9th in progression by step.

(See Deductions No. 4).

Resolutions and successions of chords of the 9th (with or without alteration of the 5th).

Study of Modern Harmony.

C V   A V   F♯ V   D♯ V

Chord of the diminished 7th in four different forms, by changing the root. This combination belongs to the classical technique, as well as to modern harmony.

DEDUCTIONS

More than ever we must remember that the generalisations which follow are deductions founded upon the work of modern composers.

(1). (A). Two chords of the major 9th of the first species, in root position, may proceed by conjunct degrees (tone or semitone) ascending or descending, by similar motion in all the parts.*

Ascending: (4), (5), (22), (23).
Descending: (1), (8), (9), (18), (26).

The best arrangement
of the parts is that of
the harmonics

(B). Two first inversions of chords of the major ninth of the first species proceed less easily under the same conditions. They are, nevertheless, (21) possible with careful disposition of the parts.

Second inversions, lending themselves to smooth arrangement of the parts, proceed easily.

Successions of third inversions under the same conditions of similar and conjunct motion, are practicable, though a little hard. (19).

---

* Notice this passage from the Finale of Franck's Symphony:

(2). (A). Two chords of the minor 9th of the first species in the root position, proceeding by conjunct degrees and similar motion in all the parts, are not very agreeable, when proceeding by whole tones. Nevertheless they may be taken by semitone (25), particularly in descending.

(B). First inversions used under the same conditions are disagreeable.

Successions of second and third inversions are not impracticable by semitone. (20).

The possibility of all these successions depends, as we have said, *on the disposition of the parts.*

(3). In combining chords of the major ninth of the first species with those of the minor ninth of the same species, some interesting progressions are found, in the root position as well as in the inversion. (19^2), (28), (29).

(4). Chords of the major and minor ninth of the first species proceed easily by major or minor thirds up or down. (3), (6), (8), (31). Besides the progressions we have pointed out, many others are possible by reason of the presence of notes common to the two chords.

The same chord of the diminished 7th may be taken in four different forms by changing the root. (32). This combination belongs to the classical technique, but the modern school draws from it new effects.

(5). The fourth inversion, which brings the ninth into the bass (forbidden in classical technique), may readily be used. (10), (11), Chap. XI (19).

In the inversions the root may be placed above the ninth, at a distance of a seventh (14), (17) (a disposition taught by Sabbatini at the end of the 18th century).

The ninth may approach the root at the distance of a second * (24).

(6). With the new resolutions given to them by the modern school, the chords of the 9th, by means of alterations,

---

* In the works of Bach, when the 8th is retarded by the 9th, this is often found approached at the distance of a second.

FERDINAND KUFFERATH.   *Ecole pratique du Choral.*

(Schott Brothers, Brussels.)

(13), (15), (25), (31); appoggiaturas (17), anticipations (13), etc., become valuable chords for harmonic research. We cannot too often repeat that the more or less agreeable sound of these progressions depends on the disposition of the parts, and also on the combination of tone qualities, if written for the orchestra.

Resolutions may be sought on all chords. (7), (16), (30.) (7). Chords of the 9th of the second, third and fourth species are not, in actual fact, used very often (7), (12); they will be used, in the future, without doubt, like those of the first species.

CHAPTER IV

PREPARATION OF DISCORDS

At the present day all discords may be approached without preparation.* It matters not what modern work we may look at to be convinced of this. We need give, therefore, but very few examples.**

SAMUEL ROUSSEAU. *La Cloche du Rhin.* (Choudens, Pubr.)
page 89.

(1) Chords of the $\frac{6}{4}$ moving a major second (or diminished 3rd) without either preparation or resolution.

page 32.

Chords of the $\frac{6}{4}$ by conjunct motion. The addition of a vocal part, nevertheless, allows of another interpretation. (See p. 32 of the Score.)

---

* For a long time there has been no question of the preparation of the minor 7th.

BEETHOVEN. *Sonata Op. 31, No. 3.*

** On referring to Chapter X (Whole-Tone Scale) there will be found examples of the augmented fifth used freely.

V. D'INDY. *Lied Maritime.*   (Rouart & Lerolle, Pubr.)

(3) $\frac{6}{4}$ chords without preparation.

CH. KŒCHLIN. *Extract from No. 4 (Epitaphe) of Etudes Antiques.*
(Suite Symphonique) (unpublished).

(4) (*a*) $\frac{6}{4}$ chords without preparation; notice also the fifths (*b*) and the false relation (*c*)).

CH. KŒCHLIN. *Le Vin.*   (Rouart & Lerolle, Pubr.)

(5) Chord of the 7th of the 4th species without preparation.

DEBUSSY. *Pelléas et Mélisande.*   Page 2.   (Durand, Pubr.)
Très modéré.

(6) (*a*) Chords of the 7th without preparation.

THE SECOND

The whole modern school seems to be hypnotised by the interval of the second, which it writes at every turn.

Some discords which were taken successively as suspensions, as resolved appoggiaturas, and lastly as unresolved appoggiaturas, have given place to combinations of frequent use. In this combination of sounds the appoggiatura is heard at the same time as the principal note, which produces the interval of a second.

The two combinations most used are:

1. The sixth added to the Common Chord; —

This must not be confounded with the chord of $\frac{6}{5}$. Here is the manner of its origin:

Suspension.   Resolved   Unresolved   Appoggiatura
Appoggiatura. Appoggiatura. sounded with
the principal
note.

2. The ninth added to the Common Chord; —

---

* We have already pointed out (page 9) this combination indicated by Père Sabbattini.

This is not a chord of the 9th, but is formed as follows:

Suspension.   Resolved   Unresolved   Appoggiatura
            Appoggiatura. Appoggiatura. sounded with
                                          the harmony
                                          note.

CLAUDE DEBUSSY.   *Children's Corner.*   (Durand, Pubr.)

(a) Appoggiatura of a Bb not heard.
(b) Gb, appoggiatura of F.
(c) Chord of Bb with sixth added; —

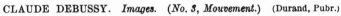

CLAUDE DEBUSSY.   *Images.* (*No. 3, Mouvement.*)   (Durand, Pubr.)

(8) Succession of chords
of +4 without 6ths, with
passing notes.

etc.

CLAUDE DEBUSSY. *Children's Corner.* (Durand, Pubr.)

(9) (*a*) F appoggiatura at same time as the principal note.

CLAUDE DEBUSSY. *Children's Corner.* (Durand, Pubr.)

(10) Common Chord with sixth added.
(*b*) Appoggiatura without resolution (see Chapter VI).

CLAUDE DEBUSSY. *Children's Corner.* (Durand, Pubr.)

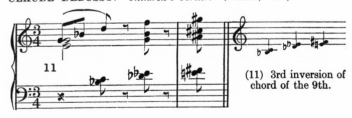

(11) 3rd inversion of
chord of the 9th.

CLAUDE DEBUSSY. *Pelléas et Mélisande.* (Durand, Pubr.)

page 143.

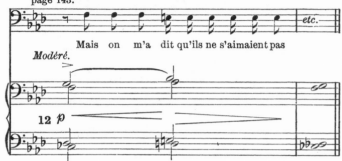

Mais on m'a dit qu'ils ne s'aimaient pas

Modéré.

12 *p*

(12) Appoggiaturas without resolution   or otherwise.

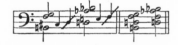

M. RAVEL. *Miroirs (Alborada.)* (Demets, Pubr.)

Assez vif.   (a)   (b)   (c)

13 *mf sec.*   (a)

(b) (c)

(13) (a) F♮ appoggiatura (on E♭) without resolution.
      (b) C♮ appoggiatura (on B♭) without resolution.
      (c) G♮ appoggiatura (on F♮) without resolution.

M. RAVEL *Miroirs (Alborada.)* (Demets, Pubr.)

(14) (a) F♯, pedal in an inner part
making the superimposed seconds:

M. RAVEL. *Miroirs (Noctuelles.)* (Demets, Pubr.)

(15) (a) Change of position in the
chord of the dominant 9th which may
even result in 3 successive seconds.

(b) Appoggiatura of the 5th resolving very correctly on the following chord. Here is the passage written in 4 parts.

RENÉ LENORMAND. *Paysage pour les Veber's.* (Rouart & Lerolle, Pubr.)

(16) Chromatic scale at the major second, which can only be explained on the ground of its humorous intention.

SAMUEL ROUSSEAU. *La Cloche du Rhin.* Page 1. (Choudens, Pubr.)

(See Chap. V.)

ANDRÉ CAPLET. *Do, ré, mi, fa, sol.* (Monde Musical, Pubr.)

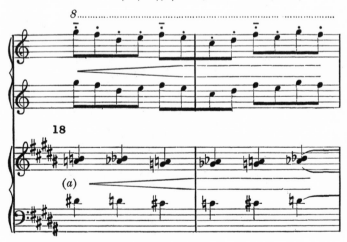

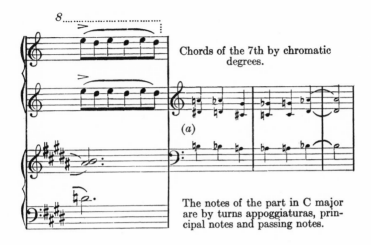

Chords of the 7th by chromatic
degrees.

(a)

The notes of the part in C major
are by turns appoggiaturas, principal notes and passing notes.

In his "Histoire de la Musique" (Vol. I, page 472), M.
Woollett quotes some curious examples from Rameau:

RAMEAU. *Platée.*

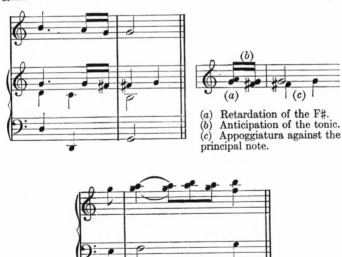

(a) Retardation of the F♯.
(b) Anticipation of the tonic.
(c) Appoggiatura against the
principal note.

(a) Ornamentation of the principal note and of a retardation of the
second.

CHAPTER V

NOTES FOREIGN TO THE CHORDS.
PASSING NOTES.   ORNAMENTS.

If fourths, fifths, sevenths, seconds, ninths may be written as harmony notes by similar and conjunct motion, one perceives that the modern school have allowed melody-notes to benefit by the same freedom.   It will be seen at the end of the chapter under what conditions they are now used.

SAMUEL ROUSSEAU.   *La Cloche du Rhin.*   (Choudens, Pubr.)

(1)   (*a*) Truncated turn in the lower part.
(2)   (*a*) Ornamentation of the major third.

SAMUEL ROUSSEAU.   *La Cloche du Rhin.*   (Choudens, Pubr.)

(3) Passing notes in augmented fourths and sixths.

SAMUEL ROUSSEAU.   *La Cloche du Rhin.*   (Choudens, Pubr.)
page 28.

(*a*) Ornamentation with inner pedal on *B*.
(*b*) Ornamentation with inner and upper pedal on *B*.

page 1.   Explanation

(a) G♮ is a passing note.

(b) C♭ E♭ G♮ passing notes.
(c) E♮ appoggiatura making its resolution simultaneously with the movement of the passing notes.

CH. KŒCHLIN. *Néère.* (Hachette, Pubr.)

(7) Ornamentation in fourths.

CH. KŒCHLIN. *Les Métaux.* (Rouart & Lerolle, Pubr.)

(8) (a) (b) Ornamentation by contrary motion (c) Ornaments making a chord of the 7th; nevertheless in the mind of the composer these combinations are written for their sonority without consideration of musical grammar.

CH. KŒCHLIN. *Berceuse phoque.* (Rouart & Lerolle, Pubr.)

(9) Passing notes in chords of the second — a rapid succession of lightly played fourths for string quartet against sustained parts for voice and flute.

CH. KŒCHLIN. *Les Métaux.* (Rouart & Lerolle, Pubr.)

(10) (*a*) F and A passing notes not preceded by the harmony note.

CH. KŒCHLIN. *Les Rêves morts.* (Rouart & Lerolle, Pubr.)

Moderato.

(11) Passing notes in 7ths.

CH. KŒCHLIN. *Berceuse phoque.* (Rouart & Lerolle, Pubr.)

(12) Passing notes in fourths and in fifths by contrary motion. This is written with the effect of the orchestration in mind.

CH. KŒCHLIN.   *Berceuse phoque.*   (Rouart & Lerolle, Pubr.)

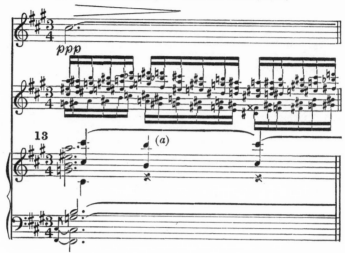

(13) (a) Passing notes in chords of the ninth. Owing to the alteration of the 5th, the character of the chord of the 9th is annulled. An
orchestral effect.

CH. KŒCHLIN.   *Accompagnement.*   (Rouart & Lerolle, Pubr.)

Mon   â - me s'ef-feuille en san - glots

(14) Simultaneous ornaments by contrary motion. (By Common
Chords.)

CH. KŒCHLIN. *Etudes symphoniques.* (unpublished.)

(15) (*a*) and (*b*) Ornamentation by Common Chords.

C. DEBUSSY. *Chansons de Bilitis.* (Fromont, Pubr.)
  Très lent. (*a*)

(16) (*a*) C♯ an auxiliary note (*b*) F✕ ornamentation below G♯
(*c*) E♯ ornamentation below F♯

ERNEST MORET. *Poème du silence.* (*Il pleut sur la mer.*)
                                      (Heugel, Pubr.)

(17) Ornamentations at the 3rd and 5th by similar motion.

E. CHABRIER. *Gwendoline.* Page 94. (Enoch, Pubr.)

(18) Chords of ⁶₄ consecutively, made by the ornaments in 4ths
(*a*) (*b*)

DÉODAT DE SÉVÉRAC.   *Le ciel est par dessus les toits.*

(a) Passing notes.

RENÉ LENORMAND.   *Paysage pour les Veber's.*

(Rouart & Lerolle, Pubr.)

(20) Passing notes in changing octaves.

Study of Modern Harmony.

(21)   (22)   Ornaments in augmented 4th and 6ths.

Study of Modern Harmony.

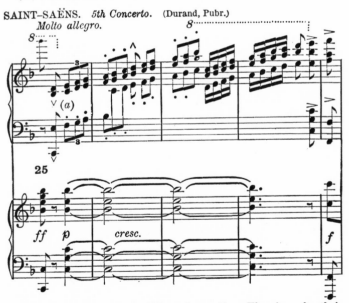

(23) Ornaments in inverted 9ths.

M. RAVEL. *Miroirs.* (Durand, Pubr.)

(24) Passing notes in 4ths.

SAINT-SAËNS. *5th Concerto.* (Durand, Pubr.)

(25) (*a*) Passing notes in fifths and sevenths. They have for their object the portrayal of an exuberance of joy, which is the character of the piece.

DEDUCTIONS

From the foregoing examples, it may be deduced that the Modern School employs passing notes and ornaments under the following conditions: —

PASSING NOTES

In seconds, in combination with appoggiaturas (6).
In minor thirds.   (Classical teaching.)
In major thirds.   Chap. X (6), (7).
In fourths (12), (24).
In fifths (12).
In augmented fifths.   Chap. X (1).
In sixths.   (Classical teaching.)
In sevenths (11), (25).
In thirds and sixths.   (Classical teaching.)
In fourths and sixths.   Chap. IV (4).
In augmented fourths and sixths (3).
In common chords (12).
In chords of the seventh (9), (13).
In chords of the ninth (13).
In changing octaves (20).
Without being preceded by the harmony note (10).

ORNAMENTS

In seconds (16).
In minor thirds.   (Classical teaching.)
In major thirds (2), (4), (5).
In fourths (7).
In fifths (15), (17).   Chap. I (7), (17).
In sixths.   (Classical teaching.)
In thirds and sixths.   (Classical teaching.)
In fourths and sixths (18).   Chap. IV (4).
In augmented fourths and sixths (21), (22).
In common chords (14), (15), (17).
In chords of the seventh.   Chap. II (2).
In inverted chords of the ninth (23).

CHAPTER VI

APPOGGIATURAS

Chord-changing, either at the same moment as the resolution of an appoggiatura, or during the continuance of the appoggiatura, is a procedure which may be found analysed in treatises on Harmony. The suppression of the note of resolution of the appoggiatura is a recent practice. This artifice opens a perspective entirely new to lovers of the unforeseen. One may thus write, by conjunct degrees, the upper or lower auxiliary of any note whatever of a chord, and then not trouble about it afterwards. . . But there must be good reason for having recourse to this means; used at all awkwardly it will easily give the impression of incoherence. Good taste alone can serve as a guide.

MAURICE RAVEL. *Les grands vents venus d'outre mer.* (Durand, Pubr.)

(1) Appoggiaturas without resolutions. (See Chap. VIII, (4) where the complete passage is analysed.)

M. RAVEL. *Sur l'herbe.* (Durand, Pubr.)

(2) Appoggiaturas without resolution.

M. RAVEL.   *Valses nobles et sentimentales.*   (Durand, Pubr.)

(3) This fragment is composed on a single chord

Let us now see the passage with the resolutions of the appoggiaturas, all of which resolutions take place only in bar *A*, where the chord changes its position:

The E (*a*) and (*b*) does not produce a change of chord. It is a passing note in both cases.

M. RAVEL. *MIROIRS (Oiseaux tristes)*. (Demets, Pubr.)

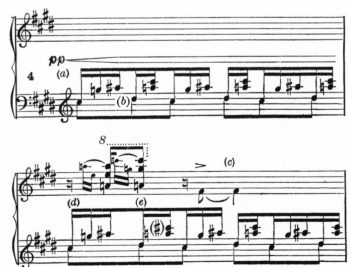

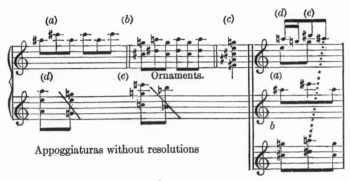

Appoggiaturas without resolutions

(*e*) In writing B♯ in place of C♮ the resolution on A♯ becomes quite natural, in spite of the presence of A♮ in the lower part, the ornamental character of which is evident.

CL. DEBUSSY.   *Chansons de Bilitis.*   (Fromont, Pubr.)

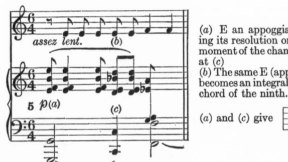

(*a*) E an appoggiatura making its resolution on D at the moment of the change of chord at (*c*)
(*b*) The same E (appoggiatura) becomes an integral note in the chord of the ninth.

(*a*) and (*c*) give

DÉODAT DE SÉVÉRAC.

(5²) See Chap. VIII (1), (2). Appoggiaturas without resolutions, or added ninth.

CH. KŒCHLIN.   *Les Rêves morts.*   (Rouart & Lerolle, Pubr.)

Moderato.

(*a*) G, appoggiatura without resolution.
(*b*) D♯ and F♯ appoggiaturas without resolutions.*
(*c*) G♮ appoggiatura without resolution.
(*d*) B, Tonic pedal.

* May be analysed classically.   See the "Traité of Reber."

CH. KŒCHLIN. *L'astre rouge.* (Rouart & Lerolle, Pubr.)

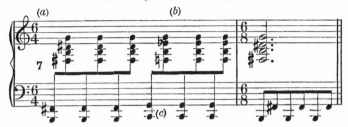

(7) (*a*) G, Appoggiatura of F♯ without resolution. (*b*) E♭ Appoggiatura of D without resolution. (*c*) Chord of the 7th over the passing tonic.

CH. KŒCHLIN. *La sommeil de Canope.* (Rouart & Lerolle, Pubr.)

(*a*) C♯ Unresolved appoggiatura of B♭.
(*b*) A♮ Unresolved appoggiatura of G.
(*c*) B♮ Appoggiatura.
(*d*) B♭ Harmony note of + 2.
(*e*) Dominant minor ninth: the G♯ should be written A♭.
(*f*) Chord of the 9th.

WOOLLETT. *Intermezzo from Sonata for Piano and Violoncello.*
(Leduc & Bertrand, Pubrs.)

(*a*) G♭ Appoggiatura of F.   (*b*) A♭ Appoggiatura of G♮.
(*c*) D♭ Appoggiatura of C.   (*d*) E♭ Appoggiatura of D♮.

CH. KŒCHLIN. *Le sommeil de Canope.*   (Rouart & Lerolle, Pubr.)

(*a*) Pedal; (*b*) F♯ passing note and ♭ ♮ of E on F♯ pedal;
(*c*) ♯♭ on F♯. (*d*) E♮ Passing note; (*e*) D♯, E♯, G♯, B♮ appoggiatura-
chord of the following chord, taken at the same time as the harmony
notes in the lower 8ve.* (*f*) The same as the previous bar.

SAINT-SAËNS. *Déjanire.* (Durand, Pubr.)

(11) Appoggiaturas in chords of the diminished fifth. They
represent the agonies of Hercules on wearing the fatal tunic.

———

* See foot-note on next page.

FLORENT–SCHMITT. *Psaume XLVI.* (Mathot, Pubr.)

(12) (*a*) E♭ appoggiatura of the D♭ in the final chord (*b*).

MOZART. *L'Enlèvement au sérail.* (Translation Durdilly.) Page 74.

The appoggiatura against the harmony note is of classical use:
    (*a*) F♯ against G.   (*b*) E against F.   (*c*) C♯ against D.
    It should be noticed that in the present case the tone-qualities are different.
    In quotation (10) the harmony notes are at the octave below.

BEETHOVEN. *Finale of the 9th Symphony.*

    Here is a characteristic example from Beethoven, in which the chord of the 7th on C♯ as appoggiatura to the chord of D minor is attacked at the same time as the latter, so that all the notes of the scale of D minor are heard together.

ALBERT ROUSSEL.   *Bourrée.*   (Rouart & Lerolle, Pubr.)

(13) Somewhat complicated as they are in appearance these harmonies
(a) (b) (c) are composed of appoggiatures of the chord of C♯ major (d).

DEDUCTIONS

1. The foregoing quotations bear specially on the unresolved appoggiatura. As we have said, the use of this
artifice depends only upon the good taste of the individual;
only musicians in whom is an artistic intuition strong·enough
to take the place of the rule should use it. (1), (2), (3),
(4), (6), (7), (8).

Chap. III (17); Chap. IV (7), (13).

2. It is evident that from the moment that it became
possible to make progressions of all kinds of harmonic
combinations by step and by similar motion of all the parts,
the modern school found itself authorised to treat appoggiaturas simultaneously by similar movement under the same
conditions of freedom.

It may be observed that if a chord is of the character of
an "appoggiatura" as regards all its notes, and if it moves
by similar motion, there results a succession of two identical
chords. The first preserves the character of an appoggiatura only by the nature of the neighbouring harmonies, or
by the presence of a pedal.

CHAPTER VII

ANCIENT DEVICES (*) { Imitations / Sequences

BAR-LINES
FALSE RELATIONS.   PEDALS
MELODIC INTERVALS

Imitations.

This artifice of traditional writing tends to disappear. Certain composers have completely renounced its use; others, and they, perhaps, form the greatest number, use it only to enhance the piquancy of the harmonic colouring.   Musicians of a classical education continue to utilise it with all the simplicity of a school exercise.   It would be as wrong to proscribe it entirely as to abuse it.   All that can contribute to the realisation of the artistic ideal conceived by the composer it is good to use. (1), (2), (3).

Sequences.

For long, in technical studies, an excessive use was made of sequences, a matter which can only be regarded as deplorable, for it inculcates in the pupil a taste for easy formulas.   The Sequence is the mother of the "Rosalia." The examples which one meets with seem to have been inspired by a recollection of the school, rather than by any æsthetic idea (7).   Nevertheless, in certain cases they may correspond with a dramatic sentiment or assist the expansion of the melodic outline.

---

* There need be no question here of the combinations, scarcely to be called musical, which entertained the masters of the XVth century. Very happily, works conceived in this spirit are to be met with only rarely in the modern period: —
    B. DAMCKE.—PRELUDE in 4 parts for organ or piano in counterpoint by retrograde and contrary motion. (Richaut, Pubr., about 1865.)
    RENÉ LENORMAND. — DIVERTISSEMENT AMÉRICAIN for piano duet in counterpoint by retrograde and contrary motion. (J. Hamelle, Pubr., c. 1875.)
    With no artistic interest this kind of music can be considered only as a virtuosity of technique in writing.

Bar-Lines.

It does not seem to us paradoxical to say that among the obstacles raised by the theorists against the development of musical thought, the most serious is that of the bar-line. It was at the outset — towards the end of the 16th century — a means of facilitating execution, and in the character of "*guide âne*," a finger post,* it rendered and still renders great services which make it difficult for us to dispense with it. But its action is not limited to these services. Little by little the notes have grouped themselves otherwise than in this bar, taking in the mind of the composer an importance relative to their position; that which precedes the bar is feebly accented, that which follows immediately is struck strongly — weak beat, strong beat. The mind of the great musicians is itself warped by the power of that habit.** The classical theorists have imposed on them the division by four measures: "The Carrure."

Without having any pedagogic intention, we counsel all young musicians to habituate themselves to think and to write without taking any account of the question of bar-lines. After that, to facilitate reading, they will add bar-lines before the accented parts of their musical discourse. From that will proceed measures of all sorts; but what does this matter?***

(See "L'Abbaye" of Koechlin, where measures of $\frac{6}{4}$ $\frac{7}{4}$ $\frac{4}{2}$ $\frac{3}{2}$ alternate, and also "Rhodante," of the same author, where are found measures of $\frac{6}{8}$ $\frac{9}{4}$ $\frac{3}{2}$ $\frac{3}{4}$ $\frac{5}{4}$ $\frac{7}{8}$ **** (8), (17).)

False Relations.

What is to be said of the false relation of the tritone? Reber found the rules "obscure and contradictory." They are now no more; no one bothers much about the false relation of the tritone. It was inadmissible that the two notes of a harmonic interval on which rested the actual tonality should be heard in two neighbouring chords. Two major thirds in succession by whole tones were forbidden,

---

* "A help to feeble minds and bad counters." Morley (Tr.).

** We may point here to the remarkable studies on Rhythm and Time of M. Jean d'Udine. We believe he is not far from sharing our point of view. In any case, his new and very personal views are of the very highest interest for musicians.

*** M. H. Woollett in his "Pièces d'étude" (Leduc & Bertrand, Pub.), gives a general list of all the bar-measures, which are to the number of fifty.

**** The Andante and Finale of the 2nd Symphony of Borodine, comprise continual changes of time.

because they produced the false relation of the tritone; for a long time major thirds *have* been so written; so we need say no more. (See Chapter X.)

The question of the false relation of the octave is more delicate; nevertheless the best authors write it, but so skilfully as to draw from it happy effects. (4), (5), (6), (9).

Pedals.*

The solid pedals of the tonic and dominant on which all the masters have piled up vivid progressions, preparations for the great climax, ingenious "stretti," etc., have not failed to come under the influence of modern times (13), (15), (16). A melodic outline may be taken as a pedal (10), (11); in other cases the pedal is so short that it may be called a "passing pedal" (12). If, in their origin (10th century), pedals were a naïve procedure for sustaining the voice,** they have become, in modern writing, a source of harmonic complexity.

(*)

GOUNOD. *Ulysse.* (Choudens, Pubr.)

Se   so - leil monte   et brû - le

This is bold harmony for the period at which it was written. We recall, to the honour of the celebrated composer, that he interested himself in musical evolution, and more than one young composer found in him a warm defender.

** Primitively the hurdy-gurdy (vielle), and the bagpipes (cornemuse) were intended to make the tonic heard in the bass, in a continuous manner; it is known that the Arabs accompanied their heroic songs with a sustained note on the Rebec.

73

EXAMPLES

G. FAURÉ. *La bonne Chanson.* (*Op. 61, No. 6.*) (J. Hamelle, Pubr.)

Allegro moderato.

(1) Imitation.

(2) Imitation.

G. FAURÉ. *La Fée aux Chansons.* (J. Hamelle, Pubr.)

Allegretto vivo (molto meno mosso)

(3) Imitation.

G. FAURÉ. *Le Parfum impérissable.* (J. Hamelle, Pubr.)

(4) False relation.

G. FAURÉ. *Les Présents.* (J. Hamelle, Pubr.)

(5) False relation.

M. RAVEL. *Miroirs.* (*Oiseaux tristes.*) (Durand, Pubr.)

The G♮ being an appoggiatura, according to classical technique there is no false relation. The same remark applies to the other chords.

S. ROUSSEAU. *La Cloche du Rhin.* (Choudens, Pubr.)

Allegro moderato.   page 118

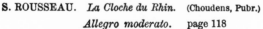
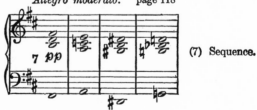

(7) Sequence.

M. RAVEL. *Sainte.* (Durand, Pubr.)

(8)   Bar of one beat.

S. ROUSSEAU. *La Cloche du Rhin.* Page 31. (Choudens, Pubr.)

(9)   (*a*) Chromatic false relation.

CH. KŒCHLIN. *Le Vaisseau.* (Rouart & Lerolle, Pubr.)
Voice & Orchestra.

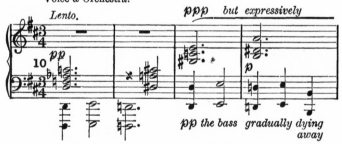

(The figure which serves as a pedal is prepared in the previous bars.)

Musical and expressive effect: drifting of the vessel, distress, soli-
tude and bitterness.

CL. DEBUSSY.   *Hommage à Rameau.*   (Durand, Pubr.)

(11) (*a*) Melodic outline forming two inverted pedals a third apart.
(*b*) Pedal in the bass.

CH. KŒCHLIN. *Soir Païen.* (Rouart & Lerolle, Pubr.)

(a) F♯ root of a chord of the 9th; (b) F♯ appoggiatura of E; A♮ appoggiatura of G; (c) B transient tonic pedal; (d) Pedals, B♭ and F.

GABRIEL DUPONT. *La maison dans les dunes.* (Heugel, Pubr.)

(13)   (*a*) A note foreign to the harmony forming an inner pedal.

GABRIEL DUPONT. *La Glu.* (ACT IV.)   (Heugel, Pubr.)

Pedal in the bass on which are imposed remote harmonies. After taking knowledge of the foregoing chapters, the reader can explain all the successions of chords by means of alterations and appoggiaturas.

M. RAVEL. *Gaspard de la nuit.* (*Le gibet*). (Durand, Pubr.)

A particularly interesting example of an inner pedal. The whole piece might be quoted, as that note, sometimes A♯, sometimes B♭, is not abandoned for a single instant, in the midst of the most disturbing harmonies, complicated by unresolved appoggiaturas.

PAUL DUKAS. *Ariane et Barbe Bleue.* Page 97. (Durand, Pubr.)

(*a*) One of the upper parts approaches the pedal F♯ from the distance of a semitone. There will be found a number of interesting examples of pedals in this score.

CH. KŒCHLIN.   *Etudes antiques No 1.*   (*Suite Symphonique.*)

(Unpublished.)

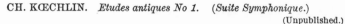

Example of changes of bars, (or rather, of phrases), written originally without bar-lines.

Melodic Intervals.

All treatises on harmony devote a chapter to the melodic intervals permitted or forbidden.

Nevertheless, the Breton labourer, the boatman on the Volga, the camel driver of the desert — to whom Nature has suggested admirable songs, as though to deride professional musicians — none of these anonymous composers have consulted treatises of harmony to know what they have the right to sing and often they have used melodic intervals said to be forbidden.

That there are some intervals more or less easy to attack is incontestable, but a "musician" will write no melodies except those possible to sing, if he writes for the voice; and in. truments do not recognize difficulties of intonation.

The question may, therefore, be looked at under two aspects:

1. In writing for instruments all intervals are accessible;

2. In writing for the voice the freedom of writing is limited only by greater or less facility of execution.

Large bodies of voices deprived of accompaniment succeed ill in enharmonic progressions.

Voices doubled by an accompaniment can approach all intervals. Voices without accompaniment, or with an accompaniment that does not double the voice parts, hesitate in approaching certain intervals.

For example, the following intervals are difficult to sing:

We may conclude that the voice is opposed to the subtleties of our system, because the same sounds (tempered) become easy to approach by changing the notation.

The composer might do well to sing all he has written for the voice, when he would be able to judge if it were possible. . . . . But there are no *forbidden* melodic intervals.

---

* The partisans of the division of the octave into twelve equal semitones do not fail to tell us that if their system were adopted these complications of Notation would no longer exist. "Nature does not know the derivative notes, and each number of vibrations produces a fundamental and unique sound, and must consequently have its own name and not be tributary to the note which precedes, or to that which follows." *Système Musical Menchaca.*

CHAPTER VIII

TO END A PIECE

The ear is so accustomed to the perfect cadence or the plagal cadence as the termination of all polyphonic compositions, that most hearers do not consider a piece finished which has not the chord of the tonic as its final chord.

Nevertheless, this commonplace close may be found to be in contradiction to what has gone before. To quote an example in a well-known piece: —

Everybody knows the admirable "Erlking" of Schubert, in which the author has shown so dramatic and poignant a sentiment. At the close of the song—where the father perceives that he has in his arms only the dead body of his son — Schubert, submitting to inexorable custom, (he must definitely finish), concludes with the most commonplace of perfect cadences.

Schumann, who was a great innovater — a fact too often forgotten — knew how to rid himself of this restraint in "The Soldier." A poor devil, in order to show himself a good soldier, carried out the order to shoot his best friend; his despair troubled Schumann, who, as a true philosopher, sees rising before him a problem of the psychology of duty; he pauses immediately, modifies the character of his harmonies and finishes on the dominant, with no tonic conclusion, making the hearer a sharer in the sentiments which animate him. The modern school has followed him in this path, and the character of that which has gone before prompts the special kind of termination to be adopted.

Here are some examples of terminations other than those made by perfect or plagal cadences.*

---

*
GOUNOD.   *Sapho.*   Page 191.   (Choudens, Pubr.)

BOURGAULT–DUCOUDRAY closes the "Rapsodie Cambodgienne" (Heugel, Publisher) on a chord of the 7̣.

DÉODAT DE SÉVÉRAC. *Le ciel est par dessus le toit.*

(Edition mutuelle.)

A finish with the 9th added to the chord of the tonic.

DÉODAT DE SÉVÉRAC. *Un rêve.* (Edition mutuelle.)

The D♯ and F♯ may be considered as appoggiaturas of E without resolution.

RENÉ LENORMAND. *Pièces exotiques.* (J. Hamelle, Pubr.)

A close with the 6th added to the chord of the tonic.

M. RAVEL. *Les grands vents venus d'outre mer.* (Durand, Pubr.)

(*a*) Appoggiatura without resolution. Interesting as a termination, this passage calls on other grounds for a careful examination.

For greater clearness, here is the harmonic progression denuded of its passing notes and appoggiaturas (in D♯ minor for simplicity).

Appoggiatura ascending and descending from the D♯ without resolution.

CH. KŒCHLIN. *L'Eau.* (Rouart & Lerolle, Pubr.)

Sixths and ninths added to the common chord, or, appoggiaturas without resolutions.

FLORENT SCHMITT. *Glas.* (Mathot, Pubr.)

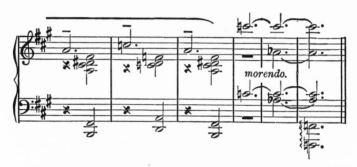

An unexpected close of great effect on the chord of F minor.

E. CHABRIER. *Le roi malgré lui.* (Enoch, Pubr.)

CHAPTER IX

SCALES — TONALITY

"The diatonic major scale may, therefore, be considered, if de-sired, as a rational product of the resonance of sonorous bodies, and having as its origin a single sound which is the base of the system; but on condition that it is regarded as a "manufactured product," of which human genius has determined the definite form according to its tastes and aptitudes."

LAVIGNAC.*
(*La Musique et les Musiciens, Delagrave.*)

"Scales do not exist; tonality alone exists and two modalities; the rest is free from all constraint."

J. HURÉ.
(*Dogmes Musicaux.*)**

"The scale does not exist. It is a formula of convention."

DERODE.
(*Introduction a l'étude de l'harmonie, Paris, 1828.*)

It is impossible to quote here all the musical scales em-ployed from the most ancient times. We will confine ourselves to pointing out those which can be utilized by the modern school, or which present some interest on the ground of curiosity.

In his "Traité d'harmonie" (Lemoine, Publisher), Gevaert gives an excellent study of the diatonic pentaphone, or penta-tonic scale. (I have adopted the French word here as being more conveniént than the rather unweildy term "pentatonic scale,") which he considers to be older than the Greek sys-tem, and which is still to be met with among the Mongols, the Chinese, the Japanese, the aborigenes of America and the Celts of the British Isles.***

---

* Among all the musicians who have expressed this opinion, we have selected a professor of the Conservatoire of Paris (M. Lavignac), a composer known for his enlightened liberalism (M. Jean Huré), and a theorist of 1830 (M. Derode).

** *Monde Musical* of July 30th, 1911.

*** Several of Wagner's themes are based on the diatonic pentaphone.

R. WAGNER. *Rheingold.* (Schott, London and Mayence, and Eschig, Paris.)

The following are different modes of the diatonic penta-phone:

These four modes may commence and finish on the dominant. It will be noticed that the scales comprise no semitones.

* * *

M. Woollett in his "Histoire de la Musique," (Monde Musical and Joseph Williams, Limited), gives us a mass of curious information concerning the ancient Hindoo scales (Volume I, page 40). It is impossible for us to write down these scales, because, except for the fifth degree, which corresponds exactly to our true fifth, all the other degrees are raised or lowered by a "srouti," an interval a little larger than a quarter tone. Some treatises of music in the Sanscrit language, dating 2,000 years before the Christian Era, disclose this system, in which the octave comprises 22 "sroutis."

* * *

If we examine the music of the Greeks, we must fix precisely the period of which we wish to speak; Greek antiquity comprises about twelve centuries during which music was continually being transformed. In the time of the Pelasgians, the scale of ¼ tones, that which constitutes the kind known as "enharmonic," was used:

¼ tone – ¼ tone – major 3rd – 1 tone – ¼ tone – ¼ tone – major 3rd.

Octave *

---

* Fétis. Preface to the 7th edition of his "Traité d'harmonie." In spite of the vast erudition of the celebrated Belgian musicographer, his assertions have been several times contested: we leave him responsible for this scale.

Later, the Hellenes, after having conquered Peloponnesus, substituted the ⅓ of the tone for the ¼ tone.

But if the oriental chromaticism spread in Greece in consequence of successive invasions, some peoples, the Dorian among others, remained hostile to the subdivision of the tone. The most ancient Greek mode that is known is the Dorian mode:

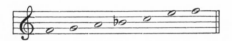

to which may be added the Phrygian mode:

and the Lydian mode:

These scales were modified and completed little by little; other modes sprang up; chromaticism and enharmonicism manifested themselves in each of these modes, only to be abandoned later; at last, in the time of Aristoxenus, the musical system of the Greeks, of a learned complexity, included 13 modes; a little later the number was increased to 15 modes, but six of these were merely transpositions*.

Leaving on one side these six transposed scales, and bringing the nine others to a uniform starting point, we have the following:**

---

* We cannot speak of Greek music without quoting the admirable studies of F. A. Gevaert: "Histoire de la Musique dans l'antiquité, Les Problèmes musicaux d'Aristotle, la Mélopée antique dans le chant de L'Eglise latine; Histoire er Théorie de la Musique grecque; Traité d'harmonie, 1st Part (Lemoine, Publisher).

** We borrow this table from the "Traité de Contrepoint" of Richter (Breitkopf & Hartel, Publishers, Leipsic).

1. Hypo-dorian or Aeolian.

2. Hypo-phrygian.

3. Hypo-lydian.

4. Dorian.

5. Phrygian.

6. Lydian.

7. Hyper-dorian or Mixo-lydian.

8. Hyper-Phrygian or Locrian.

9. Hyper-lydian.

* The sign + indicates a note added to complete the octave when the two tetrachords overlap. If the added note is at the bottom of the scale the prefix Hypo is joined to the name of the mode; if it is at the top of the scale the prefix Hyper is used.

The following are the eight Ecclesiastical tones instituted by Saint Ambrose and Saint Gregory:

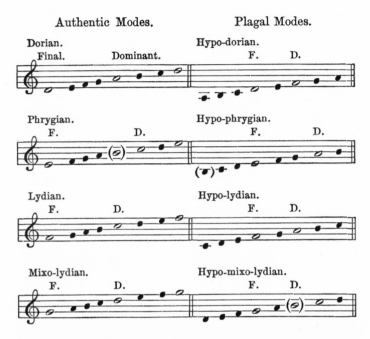

Later, six new modes were added, but two among them were found to be anti-melodic, so that four only were retained, which brought up to twelve the number of the Church tones, authentic and plagal.

Until the 10th or 11th century these modes were called 1st mode, 2nd mode, etc. Since that time the earlier Greek denominations were again used, but these have not always

been applied to the corresponding mode, an important point
for those who wish to make researches in the music of that
period.

The many scales we have enumerated offer to the composer
certain resources which can be utilised in modern polyphony.

* * *

After giving up the bizarre and monstrous hexachordal
system* musicians came little by little to use only one series,
the major scale: —

From this scale the minor scale, which appears in three
aspects, was drawn. (We leave on one side the questions
of the origins of the major and minor scales.)

Composers continually mingle these three forms.

---

* For a long period the paternity of this system was quite wrongly attributed to Guido d'Arezzo. In his "Micrologue" he says explicitly:
"There are 7 notes and we cannot have more than seven; just as after
the seven days of the week the same days repeat themselves in the
same manner as before, and the first and the eighth bear the same name,
so the first and the eighth notes must be represented by the same sign,
because we feel that they produce the same sound." ("Histoire de la
Musique moderne," Marcillac).

A very clear exposition of the hexachordal system will be found
in "La Musique et les Musiciens" of Lavignac. Page 461, (Delagrave,
Publisher).

By raising or lowering the notes of the diatonic scale we obtain the chromatic scale which may be presented under different aspects due to the notation employed.

(i) All the notes may be raised with the exception of the 6th degree which passes to the 7th by lowering this latter note:

(This scale corresponds to the major chromatic mode.)

(ii) All the notes may be lowered with the exception of the 4th degree, which passes to the 5th by an upward alteration; —

(This scale corresponds to the minor chromatic mode.)

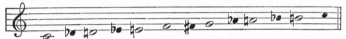

(iii) All the notes may be lowered; —

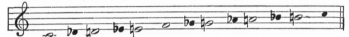

or, (iv) all the notes may be raised; —

or, (v) again, a mixture of raised and lowered notes is found; —

(a)

(b)

The chromatic scale (really imaginary since it is impracticable on all instruments with fixed notes) is therefore:

that is to say, seventeen sounds represented by twelve.

To these scales may be added many others:*

That of Hauptmann: —

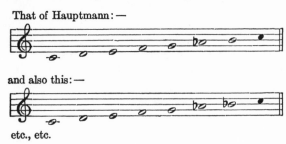

and also this: —

etc., etc.

M. Busoni, in a study on musical scales, (Breitkopf & Hartel) describes one hundred of them.

* * *

Whilst the Western races eliminated the small variable intervals, the Oriental races remained faithful to scales of one-third and one-quarter tones. The transcription of these scales is impossible by means of modern European notation — except for some which approximate to our system, but which it is necessary to say that the Orientals declare to be false when we execute them. The use of the interval of the augmented second, by which we think to give an Oriental impression, is for them a coarse proceeding, which wounds the extreme delicacy of their auditory organ.

M. Bourgault-Ducoudray in his "Mélodies populaires de la Grèce et de l'Orient," gives us an Oriental chromatic scale.

Commencing on the dominant.   Commencing on the tonic.

M. Woollett in his "Pièces d'Etudes,"** gives a table of various tonalities, from which we take the following Oriental scale:

---

* M. Anselme Vinée, in his work "Principes du Système musical et de l'Harmonie" (J. Hamelle, Publisher), brings forward an interesting study on altered scales.

** Leduc & Bertrand, Publishers.

He gives besides some examples of scales which may be formed by oneself by the mixing of tetrachords or the alteration of certain degrees.

The modern Greek Church still possesses the oriental chromaticism.

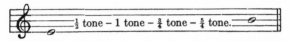

Pére Thibaut in a very interesting study* shows a comparative table of the Turkish scale — a division of the octave into 23 intervals — and the Syrian scale of Meshaqa — a division of the octave into 25 intervals.**

* * *

Modern authors make use of a scale of whole tones, which gives a succession of six notes without a leading note:

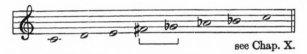

see Chap. X.

This is an important fact, because the resulting harmonic combinations destroy the shape and character of the tonality which, by comparison with the Greek tonalities, is called modern.

We have already drawn attention to the scale of M. Menchaca, consisting of equal semitones and giving a scale of twelve degrees.

M. Scriabine makes use of a scale formed from the harmonics 8 to 14, but omitting the 12th:

As a pleasantry, futurist musicians claim the use of the "commatic" scale, that is, the division of the octave into fifty-three commas. We may, without being taxed with naïveté, take this demand into consideration, because the

---

* See "La Revue Musicale S. I. M." of 15th February, 1910.

** There may be read in the "Historie de la Musique" of Woollett (Volume I) the study of the Syriac scales (Jacobite or Syrian rite) after Dom Parisot; there will be found also an interesting review of keys and modes used in the Maronite, Coptic, Abyssinian, Ethiopian and Armenian Churches.

division of the octave into small intervals is in use in the modern East. It is not a new idea; 2,000 years before Christ (see page 88), the Hindoos, futurists without knowing it, divided the octave into twenty-two "srouties." Besides, there exists in the Imperial Museum at St. Petersburg, an organ or harmonium, in which the octave is divided into fifty-three intervals; the keys are of different colours and arranged on five keyboards.

In principle we see no objection to the making of scales of small intervals, each race being free to choose the succession of sounds which best meets the expression of its sentiments. But beyond a certain limit the auditory organ can catch nothing but a confused noise.

* * *

It may be useful to recall that by tonality is meant the complete relationship established between the different elements of a series of sounds, those relationships grouping themselves around the first note of the series, the tonic.

The modern school modulates continually and with the greatest skill; the most remote tonalities are approached with facility by ingenious successions, and the change of mode which brings together more remote tonalities is always ready to come in. Besides, as the chord of the dominant seventh characterises a key, from the moment when several can be used in succession that which is called modulation — that is to say, the preparation of a new tonality — is found to be very much modified. It is no longer a group of chords that prepares a new key, it is a series of progressions of passing keys, of which the whole determines the feeling of a principal tonality.

Everybody knows that the distance from one key to another key depends upon the number of sharps and flats which differentiates them, but it must be noticed that when there are more than six sharps or flats between the two scales, they have no longer any notes in common.

In the classical style, it was considered that the keys formed upon the degrees of the diatonic scale (II, III, IV, V and VI) constituted the series of possible modulations from the principal key; the substitution of minor for major, and *vice versâ* further increased the number of these dependent keys. Now, one modulates to each degree of the chromatic scale and regards it as the tonic. Whether the composer limits himself to exploring the neighbouring keys, or whether he approaches the remote keys, he must never forget that a well-considered passage draws its value, its effect, from that which precedes and that which follows. He must never sacrifice the line of logical succession of keys and chords to the pleasure of writing a curious harmonic example.

CHAPTER X

ON THE WHOLE-TONE SCALE

This combination of notes is often used by the modern school, who draw from it curious successions of chords of the augmented fifth.*

The whole-tone scale has only six notes, and has no leading-note. It cannot terminate on the octave except by having recourse to the enharmonic.

Since it finds its inspiration in the old division of the scale into tetrachords, the whole tone scale can be divided into two tetrachords, the last note of the first being the first note of the second, which fixes the position (the 4th degree) of the enharmonic change.

---

* Wagner used chords of the augmented fifth, but most frequently by chromatic degrees, which gives them a different character from the examples quoted on pages 101 and following.

WAGNER. *Tristan und Isolde.* (Breitkopf & Hartel.)

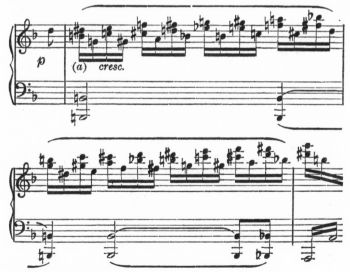

(*a*) By chromatic degrees.

In harmonising this scale we have a chord of the augmented
fifth on each degree:

In consequence of the identity of sound of the augmented
fifth and the minor sixth these chords are reduced to two:

The scale in thirds will be as follows:

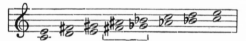

and by contrary motion:

* WAGNER.   *Siegfried.*   (Schott, London and Mayence, and Eschig, Paris.)

(*b*) By minor thirds in the bass.

We may also have the scale in chords by contrary motion:

It will be noticed that the notes of each chord of the descending scale are the same in sound as the notes of the corresponding chord of the ascending scale.

For those who are not afraid of the harshness of the discords* we may point to a curious arrangement of the scale of whole tones. In each chord the six notes of the scale are heard.

---

* The basis of the harmony of M. Scriabine's "Prometheus," is the following chord, which he treats as a perfect concord. (Nicolas Petroff. *Monde Musical* 1911) (see also Clutsam, *Musical Times* 1913. H.A.)

We are a long way from the time when the third was treated as a dissonance; besides, the classing of intervals as consonances and disconsonances is arbitrary. It may be said that, theoretically, there is but one consonance, the unison, of which the relation is represented by $\frac{1}{1}$; the farther removed from this simple relation, the less is the interval consonant, but the point where "dissonance" begins must vary according to the susceptibilities of the ear.

These combinations are not much used in the form of scales by contrary motion (11), but, taking them by themselves, one may seek and find some entertaining progressions, because each of these combinations is identical in sound with a chord of the ninth of which the fifth is doubled and altered, ascending or descending (8);

The same interpretation obtains with the other combinations.

In these scales we have indicated the enharmonic change. In practice the diminished third is approached openly:

DEBUSSY. 2

and in the scales of thirds the skip of the diminished third is made successively in the two parts, which brings about two diminished fourths in succession. See Debussy (6) and Saint-Saëns (7).

Lastly, the enharmonic character of these six chords which reduce themselves to two makes it possible to use alternatively the forms ♯₅, ₈ and ₄; Debussy (6).

There exists a second scale of whole tones; that which has for its point of departure: C♯.

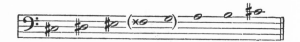

All that we have said with regard to the former scale may be applied to the latter.

There are no other whole-tone scales. Every other point of departure than C or C♯, brings about only a reproduction of these two scales.

CH. KŒCHLIN. *L'Astre rouge.* (Rouart & Lerollé), Pubr.)

Et le rou - ge Sa - hil du fond des

nuits tra - gi - ques seul fiam - be et

Explanation.

The whole on a pedal A.

CL. DEBUSSY.   *Children's Corner.*   (Durand, Pubr.)

CL. DEBUSSY.   *Prélude (piano).*   (Fromont, Pubr.)

A. BRUNEAU.   *Le Rêve.*   (1891).   (Choudens, Pubr.)

page 65.   *dolce.*

Ne craig-nez   rien   L'heure est de

CL. DEBUSSY.   *Prélude.*   (Fromont, Pubr.)

Whole-tone scale with interval of the diminished third.

CL. DEBUSSY.   *Pelléas et Mélisande.*   Page 236.   (Durand, Pubr.)

(*a*) One part makes a skip of a diminished third, the other continuing by whole tones, which gives two diminished fourths to the point where the second part in its turn makes a skip of a diminished third (*b*).

SAINT-SAËNS.   *Scherzo.*   Op. 87, page 2.   (Durand, Pubr.)

Another example of the same progressions.

H. WOOLLETT.   *Sonata in F♯ minor.*   (Leduc & Bertrand, Pubr.)
(*Piano and Violoncello.*)

An example of all the notes of the whole tone scale being heard simultaneously.   (*a*) Chord of the dominant ninth on B (in E major)

with ascending alteration of the fifth F♯ (written G for F×), and descending alteration of the same fifth F♯ (written E♯ for F♮). The ninth, C♯, approaches the root at a distance of a second which gives:

CL. DEBUSSY. *Pelléas et Mélisande.* Page 111. (Durand, Pubr.)

CL. DEBUSSY. *Pelléas et Mélisande.* Page 4. (Durand, Pubr.)

CH. KŒCHLIN. *La Guerre.* (Rouart & Lerolle, Pubr.)

Chords of the augmented fifth by contrary motion, causing all the notes of the whole tone scale to be heard simultaneously.

CHAPTER XI

VARIOUS HARMONIES

FLORENT SCHMITT.   *Tristesse au jardin.*   (Mathot, Pubr.)

Augmented eleventh.   This is the harmonic eleventh added to the ninth.

CL. DEBUSSY.   *Chansons de Bilitis.*   (Fromont, Pubr.)

(*a*) D♯ appoggiatura and afterwards ornamentation of C♯.
(*b*) A♯ and C♯ melodic
figure forming a pedal.

A♯ being equisonant with
B♭ we may also say:

CL. DEBUSSY.   *Chansons de Bilitis.*   (Fromont, Pubr.)

The transposition of the chord (*a*) readily explains this passage.
(*b*) is a second inversion of the chord of the 9th on the dominant E♭;
or a chord of the ninth, A♭ and C being appoggiaturas of G and B♭; or
still further a chord of the 11th on B♭.   (*c*) Passing notes going through
the chord.

CL. DEBUSSY.   *Chansons de Bilitis.*   (Fromont, Pubr.)

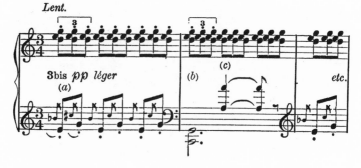

Chords are written for their sonority; it is therefore not necessary that they should all be fully explained. In the present case, the effect of the A (*c*) is so mysteriously poetic and so adequate to the sense of the words which precede that one would hardly think of asking from whence it is derived.

Nevertheless it may be said:

(*a*) 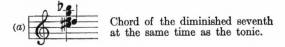 Chord of the diminished seventh at the same time as the tonic.

(*b*) D retardation of C.
(*c*) A, unresolved appoggiatura, or added sixth.

It may be interesting to analyse A as a passing note in changing octaves.

CLAUDE DEBUSSY. *Children's Corner.* (Durand, Pubr.)

Tonic and dominant pedal, with melody accompanied by the fourth below. See Chap. I, page 12, Note on Organum.

CLAUDE DEBUSSY.   *Hommage à Rameau.*   (Durand, Pubr.)

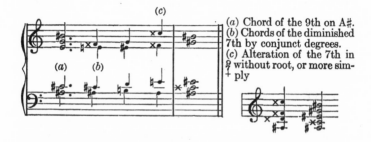

(*a*) Chord of the 9th on A♯.
(*b*) Chords of the diminished 7th by conjunct degrees.
(*c*) Alteration of the 7th in $\frac{9}{7}$ without root, or more simply

CLAUDE DEBUSSY.   *Pelléas et Mélisande.*   Page 128.   (Durand, Pubr.)

Lourd et sombre.

The explanation of passages of this kind must be sought in the sense of the words rather than in the notation of the chords. These may be explained, nevertheless, as unresolved appoggiaturas and as chords of the whole tone scale.

A. BRUNEAU. *Messidor.* Page 179. (Choudens, Pubr.)

In considering bar 2 separately we have
(b) B♭ appoggiatura of an unheard A♭, that is to say:

but if we consider bars 1, 2, 3, 4, we shall see that the first note is symmetrically the appoggiatura of the harmony note of the 3rd beat:

and we may consider the B♭ as the harmony note, the sixth replacing the 5th, or an anticipation of the 7th.

MAURICE RAVEL. *Gaspard de la nuit.* (*Le Gibet.*) (Durand, Pubr.)

Superimposed fifths.

MAURICE RAVEL. *Miroirs.* *(Alborada.)* (Demets, Pubr.)

très sec et bien rythmé

The passage transposed into D♯ minor becomes easy to analyse: (*a*) is simply an inversion of the 9th.

MAURICE RAVEL. *Miroirs (La vallée des Cloches.)* (Demets, Pubr.)

Very slow.

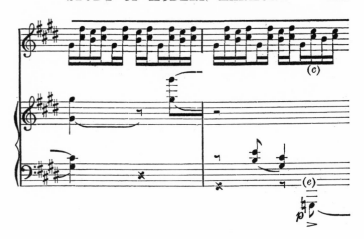

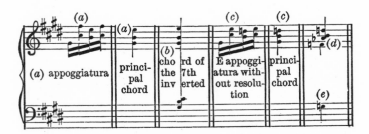

(e) G♯ root of a chord of the 9th by the equisonance of E♯ with F (d), and A♭, B and D with G♯, B and D.

V. D'INDY.*   *L'Etranger* (*Introduction to Act II.*)   (Durand, Pubr.)

The most simple combinations are sometimes of great effect. Such is the shake on G–A♭, which with the retardation below causes the following notes to be heard simultaneously.

V. D'INDY.   *L'Etranger.*   Page 85.   (Durand, Pubr.)

* See page 126.

In "horizontal" writing better count of the musical tissue can be taken by isolating the different counterpoints:

V. D'INDY. *L'Etranger.* Page 91. (Durand, Pubr.)

In music on a contrapuntal basis there is no occasion to look for the chords; what should be observed is the movement of the parts, the relation of the simultaneous sounds of which may at certain moments be classed as "chords."

In the present case we believe it to be the intention of the author to consider the bar (*a*) as being formed of counterpoints written round a single chord.

RENÉ LENORMAND. *Le Jardin des bambous.* (Heugel, Pubr.)

(*a*) Common chord with added sixth and added ninth, approached at the distance of a second.

G. FAURÉ. *La bonne Chanson.* *No. 4.* (Hamelle, Pubr.)
Allegretto quasi Andante.

Remote tonalities, lightly touching various chords.*

G. FAURÉ. *Pièces brèves.* (Hamelle, Pubr.)
Allegro moderato.

It is thus, as we have said in the preface, that M. Gabriel Fauré occupies an exceptional place by the turn, full of elegance and of modernism, which he knows how to give to successions of relatively simple chords.

---

* J. S. BACH. "A Little Labyrinth of Harmony." Works for Organ, Peters' Edition, Vol. IX.

GABRIEL DUPONT. *Les Caresses.* (Heugel, Pubr.)

The right hand plays in E minor and the left hand in C major.

GABRIEL DUPONT. *Poèmes d'Automne.* (Astruc, Pubr.)

Chords of the 6th with the bass doubled. The modern flavour
obtained by very simple means.

GABRIEL DUPONT.   *Poèmes d'Automne.*   (Astruc, Pubr.)

Et lan-gou-reu-se-ment la clar-té   se   re - ti - re: Dou-

ceur! Ne plus se voir distincts!N'etre plus qu'un! Silence!

Successions of chords of the 9th of different species in the fourth inversion.

A. ROUSSEL.   *Soir d'été.*   (*3rd part of the Poème de la Forêt.*)
(Rouart & Lerolle, Pubr.)

Explanation:

(a) Chord of the tonic of Db minor with the sixth added.
(b) 3rd inversion of the chord of the dominant 9th with the 5th altered, on Cb dominant of Fb.
(c) Chord of the dominant 7th of Db understood.
(d) Eb pedal, or merely a foreign note to the first chord.

A. ROUSSEL.   *Forêt d'hiver.*   (Rouart & Lerolle, Pubr.)

Successions of chords of the ninth (by conjunct degrees) the sixth replacing the 5th. The minor 6th being identical with the augmented 5th, the passage may be analysed as chords of the 9th with upward alteration of the 5th, the whole on an inner pedal.

A. ROUSSEL.   *Résurrection.*   (Rouart & Lerolle, Pubr.)

(a) Chord of the dominant 9th with appoggiatura.
(b) Eb appoggiatura of the 5th.
(c) Chord of the diminished 7th of the key of G minor.
(d) Tonic chord of G minor.

A. ROUSSEL. *Evocation.* (*No. 3.*) (Durand, Pubr.)

A chord built up gradually by its notes being held one after the other and embracing in its full extent the different sounds of the harmonic series.

E. MORET. *Vers tout ce qui fut toi.* (*Pour toi.*) (Heugel, Pubr.)

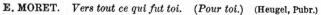

Et que j'ouvr à ge-noux pour voir comme un tré-

sor   Tout mon pas-sé dans l'ombre é-tin-celer en - cor

This composer often uses the enharmonic notation.

E. MORET.   *Une heure sonne au loin.*   (*Pour toi.*)   Heugel, Pubr.)

(*a*) B appoggiatura of A (*d*).
(*b*) D appoggiatura of the ornamental C♮.
(*c*) Ornamentation of the appoggiatura.
(*d*) A, harmony note (9th in the chord of the 9th on G♯).

E. MORET.   *Tubéreuse.*   (Heugel, Pubr.)

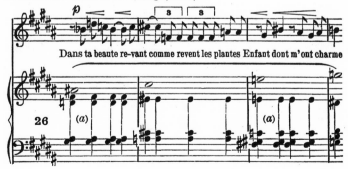

Major 9th without leading note, with downward alteration of the 5th.

CH. KŒCHLIN.   *L'Astre rouge.*   (Rouart & Lerolle, Pubr.)

(*a*) Chord of the 9th on a passing tonic.

CH. KŒCHLIN.   *Accompagnement.*   (Rouart & Lerolle, Pubr.)

Lent et très lié.

(*a*) Chord of the 7th with two appoggiaturas, A♭, C♭.
(*b*) Chord of the 13th formed by the superposition of six thirds.
(*c*) Chord of the 7th with A♭ doubled in the lower octave on E♭ pedal.
(*d*) Pedal E♭.

CH. KŒCHLIN. *Rhodante.* (Rouart & Lerolle, Pubr.)

ét sou - dain se-soulève à de-mi, pâle et som - bre

(a) Chord of the 7th on double pedal, A, E. }
(b) Chord of the 7th on double pedal Ab, Eb. } Chords having no tonal
significance and written solely for their sonority and the relation which
they have to the words.

CH. KŒCHLIN. *L'astre rouge.* (Rouart & Lerolle, Pubr.)

poco allarg. a tempo. (un peu ralenti).

The simplicity of the original harmonies of this passage is surprising.

LOUIS AUBERT. *Odelette.* (Durand, Pubr.)

(a) The voice employs the notes constituting the chord of ⁷₄ on F of the first bar.
(b) Appoggiatura.
(c) Quadruple appoggiatura of the chord of C (d).
(e) B♮ for C♭.

LOUIS AUBERT. *Préludes.* (*Crépuscule d'Automne.*) (Durand, Pubr.)

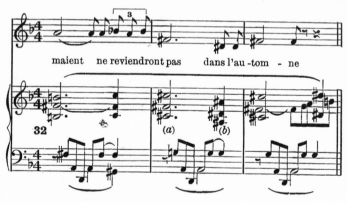

(a) Chord of ⁷₄ on A (on pedal D) F♯ appoggiatura.
(b) Double unresolved appoggiaturas:

LOUIS AUBERT.   *Nuit mauresque.*   (Durand, Pubr.)

Ma maîtres - se   tandis que l'instant se pro-

These bars, and the whole phrase that follows, rest on the chord
of $\frac{9}{7}$ on B♭. The alterations of F (F♭), and of C (C♭) are unvarying
and unresolved, giving the scale

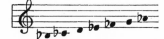

PAUL DUKAS.   *Ariane et Barbe-Bleue.*   (Durand, Pubr.)

page 87 *Lent.* (c)   (c)   (c)   (c)

(*a*) Chords of the augmented 5th proceeding by step.
(*b*) Chord of $\frac{7}{4}$ on F with altered 5th in the 3rd inversion. The E♭
afterwards becomes a pedal.
(*c*) Several interpretations are possible for the intermediate chords.
The best would be to consider them as formed of melodic notes of
different kinds.

PAUL DUKAS. *Ariane et Barbe-Bleue.* (Durand, Pubr.)
page 102.

Mon long baiser de sœur vous a-t-il fait du

cédez.

pp

35

espress.

Passage comprised in the chord of $\frac{9}{7}$ on C♯
5th altered (F× for G♮).

with the

Harmony notes:

The other notes are appoggiaturas without resolution, or passing
notes. The B♯ of the voice is borrowed for the melodic line from the
passing notes of the orchestra.

JEAN HURÉ. *Sonate pour Piano et Violoncelle.* (F♯ *minor*, 1904.)
(Mathot, Pubr.)

ppp

Lento assai.

pp

36

Example of a melody accompanied by modern harmonies. This sonata, from the point of view of the equipoise between a melody of straightforward progression and an extremely modern harmony, is worthy of note. See Chap. XII, Conclusion, page 140.

JEAN HURÉ. *Sonate pour Piano et Violoncelle.* (*F♯ minor.*)
(Mathot, Pubr.)

This fragment is readily explained by reference to Chapter X, (Whole tone scale).

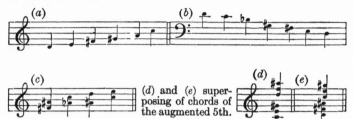

(d) and (e) super-
posing of chords of
the augmented 5th.

(See Whole-tone scale harmonized.)

JEAN HURÉ.   *Suite sur des chants Bretons.*   (1898.)   (Mathot, Pubr.)
For Piano, Violin & 'Cello.

The chord (a) may be analysed in two ways:
1. Bb appoggiatura of Ab not heard,
in a chord of the augmented 6th on Ab.

2. By taking F# as Gb, the chord
of the 9th on Ab is formed.

JEAN HURÉ.   *Sonata in F major.*   (1906.)   (Mathot, Pubr.)
For Piano & Violoncello.

Allegro ma non troppo.

The bars 1, 3 and 4 are formed of the chord of F with the 6th added; all the foreign notes are passing notes or ornamentations:

Bar 2, chord of the 9th on D♭; B♭ ornamentation: Bar 5, chord of the 9th on G♭; E♭ appoggiatura of F♭ or of the unheard D♭.

The harmonies simply stated are:

JEAN HURÉ.   *La Cathédrale.*   (Drama in preparation.)   (1910–1912.)

Quatuor avec sourdines Batterie de Cymbales pppp

M. Jean Huré has communicated to us this unpublished fragment, which defies analysis.   The chords come without doubt into the category of those written for their sonority without regard to musical grammar (?).

We observe only that in the chords (*a*) and (*b*) the same notes are heard under different conditions in changing octaves, and that the chord (*a*) sounds *all the notes* of the chromatic scale.

M. FAURÉ. *Le parfum impérissable.*   (J. Hamelle, Pubr.)
Andante molto moderato.

Mon cœur est embau - mé d'une odeur immortel   le. . .

The close of each strophe really ought to be quoted.   Moreover, the whole melody deserves to be cited as a most typical example of refined and modern expression.

ERIK SATIE.   *Le fils des étoiles.*   (Rouart & Lerolle, Pubr.)
Wagnérie Kaldéenne du Sar Péladan.   (1891..)

Prelude to 1st Act.   Prelude to 2nd Act.
En blanc et immobile.   Dans la tête.

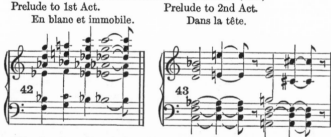

We often hear it said that the modern school, at its beginning, was inspired by Moussorgsky.   If some critics allow that line of descent, several composers affirm that they have found their point of departure in the harmonies of M. Erik Satie.   These harmonies were written twenty or twenty five years ago, in a style independent of all the technical conventions usual at the time.

Prelude to 3rd Act.
Courageusement facile et complaisamment solitaire.

Is it necessary to say that the indications of style apply to the phrases and not to the quoted chords?
This work is written without bar-lines.

We quote these harmonies, leaving the reader to estimate them to his own liking.

ERIK SATIE.   *uspud* (1892–93.)   *Ballet Chrétien.*
     Fragment from 1st Act.   (Rouart & Lerolle, Pubr.)

(a) These two last chords should be read in the G clef. According to a note by the author, this conventional style of writing has been adopted "to keep away the stupid."

ERIK SATIE.   *2nd Sarabande* (1887.)   (Rouart & Lerolle, Pubr.)

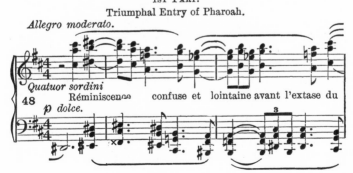

These harmonies (42) to (47), astonishing for the epoch when they were written, are readily analysed by the means which have served us up to the present.

FANELLI.(*)   *Tableaux symphoniques.*   (1883.)   (Unpublished).
     From the Roman de la Momie (TH. GAUTIER.)
          1ST PART.
     Triumphal Entry of Pharoah.
Allegro moderato.

Quatuor sordini
48   Réminiscence   confuse et   lointaine avant l'extase du
     p dolce.

Pharaon   devant   la beauté   de Tahoser, etc.

The lower parts form a succession of diminished 5ths and minor 7ths, proceeding by similar motion in all the parts, and imitating at the 7th the two upper parts. These make a succession of major thirds deriving from the whole tone scale.

" Pharoah " theme.

This passage is based on the whole tone scale.

The quotations from the works of M. Fanelli have a great interest, by reason of the period when these works were written. Composed in 1883, the first part of the "Tableaux Symphoniques" did not become known to the public until 1912!

FANELLI.(*)   *Same Work. 2nd Part, 1886.*

Dans une salle du palais. Jongleuses nues.

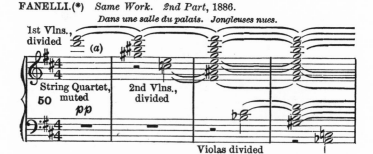

---

* M. Fanelli was born in Paris of an Italian father and a Belgian mother. He has always lived in the musical centre of Paris, and, for that reason, may be accounted as one of the French musicians.

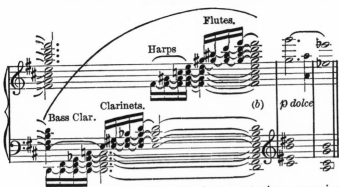

(a) The successive entries of the string instruments give a succession of major thirds by whole tones (by leaps of an octave):

(b) Chord formed by the superposition of four chords of $\frac{7}{}$ with altered fifth:

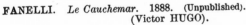

It should be noticed that the last chord G♯, B♯, D♮, F♯ is enharmonically an inversion of the first chord, D♮, F♯, A♭, C♯. By treating the notes enharmonically the chord (b) becomes accordingly a chord of the 13th with alterations.

FANELLI. *Le Cauchemar.* 1888. (Unpublished).
(Victor HUGO).

(a) Chord of the 11th with minor third.

Le monstre volant sur un lac du feu.

(*a*) Chord of the augmented 11th with altered 5th :

(*b*) Chord of the augmented 11th with altered 7th :

FANELLI. *Impressions pastorales.* 1890. (Unpublished.)

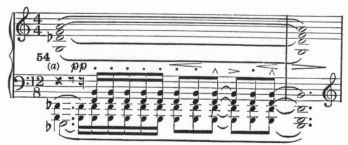

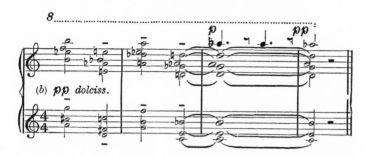

(b) pp dolciss.

(*a*) Chord of the augmented 11th.

(*b*) Chords of the 9th with altered 5th and a 13th added. Progressions by descending 5ths.

134

VARIOUS DEDUCTIONS AND REFLECTIONS

Some musicians will see in the harmonic series the indubitable origin of the chords now in use, chords which their predecessors little by little discovered by intuition. According to these musicians the origin of these chords may be established in the manner following, which leads up to the use of a chord of the augmented eleventh:*

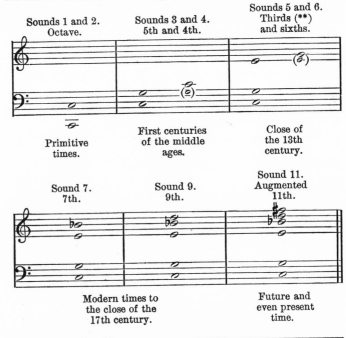

Sounds 1 and 2. Octave.	Sounds 3 and 4. 5th and 4th.	Sounds 5 and 6. Thirds (**) and sixths.
Primitive times.	First centuries of the middle ages.	Close of the 13th century.

Sound 7. 7th.	Sound 9. 9th.	Sound 11. Augmented 11th.
Modern times to the close of the 17th century.		Future and even present time.

* M. Jean Marnold, in the bulletin No. 2 of 1908 of the "Institut Psychologique," indicates very nearly the same formation of chords.

** The third, which appeared in the 13th century, was used at the same time as the fifth and the fourth in the Mixed Organum. It was objected to by reason of its dissonance. Nevertheless, Jean Cotton, who lived in the 11th century, wrote: "Master Salomon has had sung the fifth at the same point where Master Albin taught the fourth and where Master Trudon will allow nothing but the third." That seems to us to indicate that two hundred years before the date fixed by the historians, the third, in practice, was used, in the same manner as the fifth and the fourth.

Attractive as may be the interpretation given to this series of intervals, it is both disputable and disputed.*

Some say, rightly, that the sound 11 is no more an F♯ than the sound 7 is a B♭; others affirm that the formation of the chords by superposition of thirds cannot be accepted, and that the chord of the 11th cannot exist; but their opponents come forward and derive *all* chords from a superposition of thirds.

We leave the theorists to explain it among themselves and say, following M. Marnold, that M. Debussy has used the chord of the augmented 11th in "Pelléas et Mélisande." We have given an example from M. Florent Schmitt (1), and several examples from M. Fanelli (52), (53), (54).

* * *

It is important to notice that the school of which M. Vincent d'Indy is the chief, is also very modern in its manner of treating counterpoint. The means of analysis being different, the examination of the methods in use in modern counterpoint must form a separate task, though on parallel lines with the present. Notwithstanding this we have quoted several passages from M. Vincent d'Indy, because it is impossible to write a work on modern music without naming this eminent composer; his place would be momentous in an analytical study of works characterised more by "horizontal" writing than by "vertical" writing. (12) and (13).

* * *

All the foregoing quotations bear upon harmonic facts typical of modern writing; their character from the point of view of "composition" has not been considered. There is no need to dissimulate the fact that all these peculiarities of writing, interesting in themselves, are nothing if they do not enter into the logical development of a musical thought. Perhaps it may be a reproach to some musicians that they have allowed themselves to be seduced by the search for rare phenomena, to the detriment of inspiration.

We often meet with works so bristling with interesting harmonies that emotion is practically excluded. Here we have a stumbling-block which true musicians will know how to avoid. Moreover, it would be rash to pass judgment on the sincerity of the emotion of modern composers, and a musician who is accused of "gratuitous complication" often only shows a very sincere sensibility, in a form which to him has become familiar and personal.

---

* In the "Principes du Système musical et de l'Harmonie" of M. Anselme Vinée (J. Hamelle, Publisher), read his theory of chords.

* * *

New systems develop themselves from different sides.*
Some are based on the harmonic series, others on the division
of the octave into small intervals, while still others bring the
division into twelve equal semitones.   The partisans of this
last division have not failed to notice that modern composers
often write ♯ for ♭ and *vice versa*, as the two notations indicate

---

* We have said in the notes on page 8, that finding his works un-
intelligible, we have scarcely ventured to quote Mr. Schoenberg, of
Vienna.   Two bars from that author will suffice to explain our reserve.
Mr. Schoenberg is a professor at the Conservatoire at Vienna.

ARNOLD SCHŒNBERG.   *Drei Klavier-Stücke.*   (Universal Edition.)
Op. 11, No. 3.

the same sound. Chap. XI (10), (20), (24), (26); Chap. VI (4), (8), etc. Still further, in certain scores may be found a phrase with sharps in one part, and the same phrase with flats in another part, moving at the octave, or in unison with the first.

* * *

It will occur to no one to deny to the older technique the possibility of chromatic and complicated harmonies. On that subject one may re-read Bach, Schumann, Chopin, as well as Wagner, who by comparison is allied with the older music rather than with the modern music. As to Beethoven, he seems to have concerned himself little with harmonic research; in the complete power of his genius, he gave himself to the development of ideas. This attained such greatness that the piquancy of uncommon harmonies became useless. Nevertheless, he never drew back from any harmonic boldness of which he had need for the interpretation of his thought.*

---

* We have already quoted the opening of the Finale of the 9th Symphony (note, page 68). Here is another example from the Finale of the "Pastoral" Symphony. Fètis, as a good professor of harmony, corrected this passage, "that mistake (!) of a great artist." This fragment is usually analysed as an entry of the Horn in the key of C on a pedal on F. We cannot refrain from considering the G as a retardation of A.

We quote further the following passage from the 5th Symphony, which brought against Beethoven the most bitter criticisms on the part of professors of harmony; —

Composers of classical education may write in modern harmonies,** their technical skill permitting them to attack every variety of form.   Do they then perform this as an act of freewill, or do they involuntarily fall beneath the influence of the atmosphere of to-day?   It is a difficult point to decide.

Besides, in seeking an answer to our question, we may find that certain authors are modern only in their *wish* to write remote harmonies, and are not led to do so by their natural feeling.

Foot-note to p. 137 (cont.)

** THÉODORE DUBOIS.   *Promenade à l'étang.*   (Heugel, Pubr.)

* * *

In this short review of the harmonies employed to-day, we have not been able to quote all composers, and we have not always given to those that we have quoted the important place which is due to them.   We have to ask of them all not to see any partisanship in our silence or our reserve.   The works available in our library have alone determined the choice of quotations.   These have been made in a spirit of entire impartiality, without taking any account of our own preferences.

CHAPTER XII

CONCLUSION

When it is seen that each of the passages quoted may be explained by means of the older technique, the reader may be tempted to conclude that modern harmony is no other than classical harmony treated with greater liberty. This would not be quite exact. Strictly speaking, nearly all the new music can be analysed with the aid of the older treatises on harmony and counterpoint, modern authors having all made classical studies, the minds of the greatest innovators bowing involuntarily to the indelible influence of that teaching. It therefore results that in the most modern music we may nearly always recognise, in spite of dissimilarity, the strand which connects it with the classical technique.

Nevertheless it seems to us that there is in this music a new harmony in a latent condition, which ere long will break that strand, which will throw down the ramparts with which the professors of harmony have involuntarily encircled the ancient teaching.

If we have been able, not without a certain feebleness, to analyse some bars of modern music, artists will be quick to perceive the insufficiency of our commentaries. A new technique is required for modern thought. It will not be formulated, we believe, except by an artist having the power to develop himself outside the schools, and it will depend on the position taken by the theorists with regard to the origin of the notes.

To establish a system we must lean upon something that is stable; but to-day, we are in the presence of three series of notes which, at every instant, mix themselves in a most illogical manner; — Pythagorean notes, natural notes and tempered notes. Choice must be made eventually, and the theory of harmony brought into line with the instruments.

In our preface we examined the different routes which may be followed by composers in a future time. Without taking any side in the question, we may notice that the theoretical division of the octave into twelve equal semitones has nothing illogical about it, seeing that it exists in practice, by the use of the instruments of fixed sounds, and that our composers manifest more and more a kind of indifference in the choice between ♯ and ♭.*

---

* We have found examples of this in our best modern authors, who cannot be taxed with ignorance.

In expressing this opinion we desire to give rise to useful discussion, and have no intention of extolling any new system. Any other technique which will abolish the absurdity of writing a music which cannot be executed, and which will open a wider path for the evolution of to-day, must excite the interest of all musicians.

But, it will be said, this will make it necessary to modify the theory of music! We do not ask for this, but, why should not such change be made? Did the Greek system prevent the theorists of the Middle Ages giving us the hexachordal system? And has this hindered the genesis of our present system?

And do they really imagine that this last must remain to the end of time? This would surely be too naïve.

At the present time, we have, old and young, been "moulded" by a traditional technique, which does not leave us at liberty to invent another. To the musicians of to-morrow belongs the task of building a new musical system responding to the needs of composers' thoughts. The music of to-day will be an excellent preparation. To suppose that melody will disappear in the midst of harmonic complications is, we believe, an error. At first, that complication will exist only for musicians of an incomplete education, and afterwards, we may be certain that the melody will extricate itself as readily from the modern harmonies as it has extricated itself from the harmonies of Schumann and Wagner. These, to a contemporary of Mozart, would pass for veritable ramblings. . . Besides, was not Mozart accused of lack of melody, in spite of the simplicity of his harmonies?

Let modern musicians write but the music of their period* and they will have fulfilled their duty as artists. The example was set them by Schumann, Chopin, Wagner; Liszt, Berlioz, Saint-Saëns, etc., who, at the suggestion of their surroundings, broke the classical moulds in order to formulate a music adequate to their mentality. The musicians of the school of to-day have followed them in this way.

---

* One conceives that the older artists whose efforts were worthy of admiration, but who remained enclosed in the circle of the studies of their youth, must be displeased at seeing a new art brought to birth, an interpreter of a mentality which is no more theirs and which they cannot, or will not, understand. An old composer, of a humorous turn of mind, once said to us: "In my youth, there were two kinds of music, good and bad; the situation was very simple; one stood for one or for the other. Modern composers — men of great talent — have invented a third kind of music: disagreeable music . . . One no no longer knows which side to take."

But if the masters whom we now quote freed themselves from conventional forms, they did not change the musical language in any radical fashion.

On the contrary our modern composers have completely modified the harmonic idiom at the same time as the form.

We may say also that modern works give us impressions of subtlety and charm more often than impressions of power and grandeur. Must we conclude that the technique of which we have quoted so many examples does not lend itself to the construction of powerful and developed works? Certainly not; we could point to compositions of the new school where these qualities are to be met.

This school has just made a great effort to free itself from the past; we must give it time to take advantage of its conquests and to produce the works which we have a right to expect from it. . . .But if this new art be only a refinement of the older art, arrived at the end of its evolution, the perpetual advancement of the art will not be arrested, and we should see new formulas arise of which we cannot at present foresee the character.*

RENÉ LENORMAND.

---

* At the beginning of this study we predicted the coming of new treatises of harmony; since the time when the principal parts of this work were written, new theories of music have made their appearance:
Principes du Systéme musical et de l'Harmonie, by Anselme Vinée.
Traité d'harmonie ultra moderne, by Louis Villermin.
I Moderni orizzonti della tecnica musicale. Teoria della divisione dell'ottava iu partiug uali, Domenico Alaleona (Torio. Fratelli Bocca, pubrs., 1911).

A STUDY OF

Twentieth - Century Harmony

A TREATISE AND GUIDE
FOR THE STUDENT - COMPOSER OF TO-DAY

by

MOSCO CARNER

VOLUME TWO—CONTEMPORARY HARMONY

LONDON : JOSEPH WILLIAMS LIMITED
29, ENFORD STREET, MARYLEBONE, W.I.

Made and Printed in Great Britain

To

My Dear Parents

PREFACE

The present book is a sequel to Lenormand's *A Study of Modern Harmony*, which was written as early as 1913 and is, in the author's own words, "almost exclusively French in its scope." Since those days music has undergone many changes in both its technical and aesthetical aspects, and new problems have arisen— some of them still waiting for a satisfactory solution. Its whole organism as it appeared to preceding generations of musicians seems to have altered radically during the last few decades. Tempting as it would be to relate these changes to similar ones in the other arts, and to look for their common causes in the transformations that have taken place in our general spiritual and material life since the last war, we still lack the necessary perspective for such a task.

In our art, none of its various technical elements have been more affected by this evolution than harmony and tonality. It is with these two, closely related to each other, that we shall here concern ourselves. This book is in the first place an attempt to put on record the changes that have occurred in these two domains, and to point to those problems which in the writer's view have been chiefly responsible for the new aspect of harmony and tonality in modern music. To survey the scene of contemporary music with its various "isms"—impressionism and expressionism, chromaticized diatonicism and diatonicized chromaticism, polytonality and atonality and what-not—is like gazing at the changing colours of the kaleidoscope. Hence the difficulty of presenting a study of contemporary harmony in such a manner that the student-composer, to whom this volume is chiefly addressed, will be able to see the main channels of modern harmonic evolution and not lose his way in the maze of of its many details.

I have therefore divided this book into three principal parts. The first discusses by way of introduction the three great problems of harmonic evolution in general. The second is devoted to the chord as such, *i.e.* its basic structure, and the modifications of this structure by chromatic alteration and the modern treatment of the unessential notes. Finally, in the last part an attempt is made to examine those powerful influences, which the break-up of classical tonality, chromaticism, the introduction of new scales, and with it, the appearance of new concepts of tonality, have exercised over the field of modern harmony. I have tried, wherever and whenever possible, to point to historical precedents and to set the various phenomena against their historical background. I have also endeavoured to show how most of them are the natural outcome of an evolutionary process. It is for these reasons that I interpreted the term 'contemporary' in a broader sense than usual, covering by it not only the last two or three decades but the period of the last fifty years or so. For the seeds of some of the most recent developments are to be found in the music between 1890 and 1910, and even earlier.

Considering the complex nature of the subject and the chief purpose of this book, I found it at times necessary to repeat certain points for which I beg the reader's indulgence.

I take here the opportunity of acknowledging my thanks to Messrs. Boosey & Hawkes, the Oxford University Press, Augener, Ltd., Messrs. Novello & Co. Ltd., Messrs. J. & W. Chester, Messrs. J. Curwen & Sons, Ltd., Messrs. Murdoch, Murdoch & Co., Universal Edition (London), Messrs. Schott & Co Ltd. (London), A. Fürstner (London), G. Ricordi & Co. (London), Messrs. Hug & Company (Zurich), and the Music Library of the British Broadcasting Corporation for their kindness in lending me most of the necessary music, and for giving me permission to quote from it. I also wish to express my sincere gratitude to my friends, Mr. Ralph Hill and Miss Enid Simon, for reading the proofs of this book.

M.C.

London, January, 1942

CONTENTS

Copyright 1942 by Joseph Williams Limited,
29, Enford Street, Marylebone, London, W.1.   W. 470   All rights reserved

PART I.

CHIEF PROBLEMS OF HARMONIC EVOLUTION

TAKING a bird's-eye view of a thousand years of harmonic evolution—from the time when Western musicians first tried to combine sounds of different pitch and grope after the natural harmonic laws of our sound-material, up to the present day when every one of these laws seems to have been abandoned and harmony appears to be no longer guided by an overriding principle of general validity and application—the keen observer is bound to detect three chief problems that have occupied Western composers and musical scholars at all times. They are the relation between consonance and dissonance, the balance between horizontal and vertical polyphony,* and the setting up of tonal centres commonly described as tonality. The solutions of these problems have been different at different periods of our musical history and have so vitally influenced the course of harmonic evolution that they represent in fact the main stream in the general history of harmony.

Let us consider, first, the relation between consonance and dissonance, or, to put it differently, the fixing of the norm of dissonance. This problem is but a special manifestation in the realm of music of a general psychological phenomenon that accompanies our whole mental, emotional and physical life. It is the phenomenon of tension and relaxation. Our life processes are governed by it in the same way as the "life" of the sea is governed by high and low tides. The sea constantly at low tide is dull and lifeless; life without tension—if this were possible at all—may appeal to the philosopher or esoteric but it would be insipid and tedious to most of us.** And so it is with music. Music without dissonances is monotonous and aesthetically most unsatisfactory *** What gives life to music is movement, and musical

---

* Throughout the book the term "polyphony" is used in its strict sense denoting music that consists of a simultaneous combination of sound as opposed to single-line music such as the Gregorian Chant.

** This is what Goethe meant with his "Alles in der Welt laesst sich ertragen, nur nicht eine Reihe von schönen Tagen" (Anything in this world is easier to bear than a succession of lovely days.)

*** That this notion is by no means of recent origin is shown, for instance, in a passage from Charles Burney's *The Present State of Music in France and Italy* (1771). Burney writes: "No one will, I believe, at present deny the necessity of discord in the composition of music in parts; it seems to be as much the essence of music, as shade is of painting; not only as it improves and meliorates concord by opposition and comparison, but, still further,

movement is born not only of rhythmic energy but also of the interplay of dissonance (tension) and its resolution, the consonance (relaxation). Just as our life processes are dependent on the "right" proportion between tension and relaxation so is musical movement largely dependent on the "right" ratio between dissonance and consonance.

But what is this "right" ratio? Is there a precise and always valid answer to this question? The history of harmonic evolution is to a great extent one long and continual attempt to provide this answer. Many answers, it is true, have been found but none of them was of such a nature as to hold good for all styles and periods. No particular fixing of this "right" ratio between dissonance and consonance was fundamental or final at any particular phase of harmonic evolution. The reason is that there is no absolute standard or norm by which to distinguish and separate dissonance from consonance. There is, only a relative norm or, in other words, our distinction between dissonance and consonance is based upon a constantly changing perception of satisfactory and less satisfactory sound combinations. In fact, the theory of the so-called beats or throbs, which are the result of the discrepancy in the vibration numbers of two notes of different pitch, has shown that, with the exception of the octave, there is no interval of an absolutely concordant nature. Even the time-honoured concords of our text-books—the perfect fifth and fourth, the major and minor third—are discords in that they have a proportionally varying degree of harshness owing to the presence of more or less perceptible beats. And it is this degree of harshness that determines our mental impression of satisfactory and less satisfactory intervals. No strict line can, therefore, be drawn between consonance and dissonance. The clear distinction of classical harmony between consonance and dissonance was really fictitious, as the theory of the beats has proved, and is, as modern music exemplifies, being gradually replaced by a sliding scale of discords of varying degree. It has taken musicians well over a thousand years to discover the relative nature of concords

---

as it becomes a necessary stimulus to the attention, which would *languish over a succession of pure concords* (my italics). It occasions a momentary distress to the ear, which remains unsatisfied, and even uneasy, till it hears something better; for no musical phrase can end upon a discord; the ear must be satisfied at last. Now, as discord is allowable, and even necessarily opposed to concord, why may not *noise*, or a seeming jargon, be opposed to fixed sounds and harmonical proportion? Some of the discords in modern music, unknown till this century, are what the ear can just bear, but have a very good effect as to contrast. The severe laws of preparing and resolving discord, may be too much adhered to for great effects; I am convinced that provided the ear be at length made amends, there are few dissonances too strong for it." (Quoted from *The Music Lover's Miscellany*, selected and edited by Eric Blom, Gollancz, Ltd., London, 1935.)

or discords—it all depends which side of this sliding scale one looks at—and it is this phenomenon that made it impossible to find a generally valid answer to the question of what is this "right" ratio between consonance and dissonance. Every period had its own proportion, every period had its own fixing of the norm of the dissonance, and every period thought of its own norm as absolute.

In this process of finding the norm of dissonance, another general phenomenon is noticeable: the dissonance, the "foreigner", becomes gradually acclimatised among the consonances, its "hosts", and thus loses its former dissonant character. In other words, the musical ears of one generation became gradually accustomed to what the preceding generation considered as a harsh dissonance with the result that the former discord was now accepted as a concord. Think, for instance, of the interval of the minor third which medieval music considered for a long time as a discord, and as late as Bach's time this view manifested itself in the avoidance of a minor third at the conclusion of a piece in a "minor" mode or a minor key, and in its replacement by the major third, the so-called *Tierce de Piccardie*, or simply by ending on the bare fifth. In Haydn's and Mozart's time there was no longer any doubt as to the concordant nature of the minor third. The history of the perfect fourth (see p. 17) is another example of the changeableness and instability of such norms.

It is clear that this constant process of "acclimatisation" of the dissonance necessitated a corresponding raising of the norm. If the dissonances were in course of time accepted as consonances by the musical ears of successive generations, and if harmonic movement was to be kept going, the increase both in number and degree of new dissonances was inevitable. Given a certain period in musical history with its norm of dissonance, the subsequent period had, in order to satisfy its own sense and feeling for dissonance, to raise that norm and seek discords of a higher degree of harshness than that which was considered in the previous period as the utmost limit. The seventeenth century was loath to use the triad with a minor third at the conclusion of a piece because its norm of dissonance was very low. The eighteenth century raised this norm so that the minor triad and its inversions were included in the family of concords, and the nineteenth century again raised this norm so that dominant sevenths and diminished sevenths came under the category of concords or, rather, satisfactory discords that required no resolution. This process continues in present-day music, which has reached such a high pitch of dissonance that all the former discords of classical and romantic harmony have come to be regarded as more or less satisfactory in themselves, and that only an orgy of dissonances can now satisfy our demand for dissonant sound-combinations. Hence, the gradual replacement of the common triads, first by dominant sevenths, then by other fundamental discords, and finally by any dissonant chord formation, the intensification of chromatic alterations, the ever-increasing use of the dissonant unessential notes, and the ruthlessness with which the modern style of horizontal writing is used in order to produce harmonic clashes of the utmost violence.

But in spite of all this the fundamental law of tension and relaxation is still making itself felt. It manifests itself in the fact that dissonances of a higher degree are often followed by dissonances of a lower degree of harshness, thus creating the feeling of relieved tension, and relative resolution of the higher dissonance. But there is one thing to be considered in this kind of resolution if we compare it with the resolutions of traditional harmony. Take, for instance, the following chord progression :

No. I.

It is obvious that the first chord possesses a higher degree of dissonance than the second. Both chords are discords from the point of view of traditional harmony, yet every musician will agree that by resolving the first chord on to the second the harmonic tension has decreased; but if we are confronted with such modern chords as in the next example :

No. 2. BERG, Wozzek (Act I).

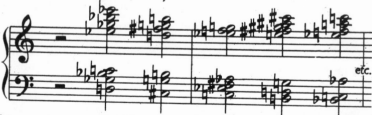

how are we to tell with any measure of accuracy and certainty which of these chords possess a higher and which a lower degree of tension or dissonance? Is not the very fact that in analysing modern harmonies we have to pose this question continually—a question that can hardly arise in classical music—a strong proof that modern music is still waiting for its norm of dissonance to be established? It would seem that nowadays every composer has his own private norm, as it were, and that, according to it, he determines which interval or combination of intervals, i.e. chords, have for him a higher and which a lower degree of tension. (In a later chapter reference will be made to the attempts of Křenek and Hindemith to guide the student in this maze of modern dissonances.)

We have to admit that both the absence of such a fixed norm of dissonance and the extremely discordant nature of modern harmony in general represent the main stumbling-block for most people who want to arrive at an unbiased judgment of the music of their own day. But it would certainly bring them a step nearer to it if they realised that the present state of flux can only be temporary and that on the strength of historical analogies it will sooner or later crystallise into a more orderly and stabler condition. Besides, this state of affairs is only the natural outcome of an evolutionary process which in the last resort is, as I have tried to demonstrate, determined by psychological laws to which our whole life is subject.

Towards this evolutionary process the public has always at first reacted unfavourably. It seems that, generally speaking, our musical ears are much more sensitive to the vertical factor than to any other in music. We are inclined to tolerate and accept much more readily melodic boldness and rhythmical extravaganza than harmonic innovations. The history of harmonic evolution bears this out in a convincing manner. In the fourteenth century Jean de Muris complained in his Ars Contrapunti of the use of new dissonances; at the beginning of the seventeenth century Monteverdi shocked his contemporaries with his harmonic audacities; Beethoven was criticised for the harshness and stridency of his harmonies in the Eroica; Wagner's harmonic innovations were regarded as scandalous; Strauss's Elektra was, I believe, responsible for the introduction of the term 'cacophony' into the jargon of musical criticism;* and at a performance in Vienna of Křenek's opera Jonny spielt auf, at which the writer was present, a certain clique in the audience showed their lack of appreciation in an unorthodox manner by throwing stink-bombs and letting loose white mice. Indeed, the story of scandals and press battles after performances of certain works by Schönberg, Berg, Webern, Bartók, Stravinsky and others would fill volumes.

So much for the dissonance. Let us now turn to our next problem : the balance between horizontal and vertical writing. Ever since the beginning of Western music, the pendulum has kept swinging between these two possibilities. First we had pure and simple horizontalism in the single-line melodies of ancient Greek Music**and the Gregorian Chant. This period lasted roughly 1400 years (600 B.C. to 800 A.D.). Then came

---

* There is an amusing cartoon made at the time when Elektra had just come out. It shows the scene of an execution at which the wretched delinquent is gradually tortured to death by the sounds which Strauss in the role of an executioner-cum-trumpeter blows into his head. In his left hand, Strauss is seen holding the score of Elektra.

** The attempts of the ancient Greeks at some sort of horizontal polyphony, the so-called heterophony, was hardly of any consequence. (See p.56)

the discovery of polyphony born of the attempt to sing the same melody simultaneously at a different pitch.* The result was the first, though extremely crude form of horizontal polyphony: the *organum* and the faux-bourdon, producing the first harmonies such as perfect fifths, the perfect fourths, major and minor thirds, and their respective inversions. (This was only natural as the two notes forming the perfect fifth and the major third stand in close acoustical relationship to each other and constitute the overtones best heard in the harmonic series of any given note. Musical instinct began to grope after the natural harmonic laws.)

Out of this primitive form of polyphony grew a more elaborate kind of horizontal writing—the descant—which led from the *ars antiqua*, as exemplified in the music of the Notre Dame School, to the Italian *ars nova* of the fourteenth century, the early English and Elizabethan music, the Netherland composers, and finally to Orlandus Lassus and Palestrina with whom the pendulum reached the middle point on its way to vertical polyphony. A characteristic of the harmony of this period, which lasted roughly 800 years (800 to 1600 A.D.) was that it resulted more or less by accident from the simultaneous singing of two and more parts. This is what Zarlino, the great Italian theoretician, meant when he said in his *Istituzioni Harmoniche* (1558) that "*l'harmonia nasce dal cantare che farno insieme le parte.*" ("harmony is born of the singing together of the parts"). During the following hundred and fifty years the pendulum had swung so far towards vertical polyphony or homophony, as it is frequently called, that in 1722, Rameau was able to state the very opposite of Zarlino's dictum when he said in his *Traité de l'Harmonie* that "*la mélodie provient de l'harmonie*" ("melody originates in harmony").

During this period the six modes, the tonal basis of the music up to about 1600, had gradually become obsolete and their place was now taken by the diatonic system with only two fundamental modes or scales, the major and the minor. Upon this new tonal basis a harmonic organisation was set up in which the common triad constituted the nucleus of all other chord formations. Moreover, every note, every chord and chord progression, and every key of modulatory schemes stood here in clearly defined relation to a centre and, through it, to one another. This is what we mean by functional harmony, with the tonic, dominant and sub-dominant as its pivots. The period in which this system reigned supreme was the eighteenth and the first half of the nineteenth centuries. Its chief landmark was the homophonic music of the

---

* Single-line horizontalism seems to represent the very first stage in musical development. Polyphony, whether horizontal or vertical, argues already a capacity for correlating sounds of different pitch—a capacity which, as the modern psychology of the child and of primitive tribes has shown, points to a later and higher stage of general intelligence.

great Viennese school. It is upon the harmonic language of this period that our text-books on harmony are based.

The culmination point of vertical polyphony was, however, reached in the works of the later Wagner and the later romantic school, such as Wolf, Bruckner, Mahler, Strauss, Reger, Schreker, Delius, the French Impressionists, and the early style of some modern composers, such as Schönberg, Berg, and Stravinsky. This development which may be said to have terminated with the war of 1914-18 represents the harmonic period in our musical history. It is the period in which every possibility of vertical construction was exploited to the full. The chord as such became an end in itself. Its *raison d'être* lay not so much in its function as vertical support of the melody as in the mere sensation of sound it was able to create. The degree of tension and the tonal colour, which partly depends on it, were the chief criteria that guided composers in their harmonic technique.*
This explains the growth, during this period, of chords into clusters of notes—often veritable chordal monstrosities—taking the place of the simple three- and four-note chords of classical harmony. And as harmonic tension and tone-colour are, apart from particular methods of instrumentation and of lay-out which we will consider later in the book, dependent upon the degree and intensity of dissonance it becomes clear why this period had to resort to novel chord formations that showed any possible combination of dissonant intervals, and that were no longer exclusively based upon the principle of superimposed thirds. In this we can clearly see the close interplay between the problem of dissonance and that of vertical polyphony. This strongly pronounced cultivation of the chord *qua* chord also explains the abundance of chromatic alterations, unresolved suspensions and appoggiaturas, anticipations, passing-notes, and free pedals in the bass and middle parts, all of which were frequently combined to produce vertical associations of the strangest sound and colour. In fact, the simultaneous use of all these devices constitutes a most important characteristic of the harmonic style of this period and largely accounts for its complex nature.

While this process was still in full swing the reaction against it set in. Verticalism had reached a state of hypertrophy. The pendulum began to swing back again to horizontalism, yet a horizontalism that stood many points higher on the evolutionary spiral than that of the period between 800 and 1600. This new horizontalism is the so-called linear style of modern music. Its beginnings were already discernible in the works of the very

---

* The relation between overtones and tone-colour must, of course, not be forgotten.

same composers who cultivated extreme verticalism. The polyphony of Wagner's later works, such as *Tristan*, *The Mastersingers*,
and above all *Parsifal*, contained, though born of harmony, the
seeds of the coming linear style of fifty years hence. Strauss,
Mahler, Reger, and the early Schönberg show in their works
chordal structures of utmost complexity cheek by jowl with
contrapuntal lines that are set against each other with little
regard for the vertical result. And composers such as Bartók,
the later Stravinsky, the later Schönberg and his school,
Hindemith, Milhaud, Křenek, Toch, Szymanowski, and many others
further developed this modern form of contrapuntal writing with
complete disregard for the harmonic clashes it produced.

From this it was but a step to multiple*tonality (bitonality
and polytonality) in which the various contrapuntal strands of
the musical texture belong to different keys and thus move on
different. tonal planes. The extreme verticalism of the years
between 1890 and 1910 was followed by the extreme horizontalism
of the period lasting roughly from 1918 to the middle Thirties.
Its violently discordant character was a measure of how high the
norm of dissonance had been raised since the time when, even
thirds were regarded as discords. Thus we see again the close
interplay between the problem of dissonance and that of the
balance between horizontal and vertical polyphony.

Yet the verticalism of the preceding period was not entirely
dead. It manifested itself in a new technique. This was the
contrapuntal combination of chordal streams: instead of single
lines, fully harmonised melodies were set against each other,
producing streams of chordal blocks which greatly increased the
intensity and violence of harmonic clashes. But again it was the
horizontal factor that mattered.

And now for our third and last problem: tonality. Ebenezer
Prout, in his *Musical Form*, said that "without clearly defined
tonality music is impossible". This was written in 1893 when
multiple tonality and atonality were undreamt-of things. The
conception of tonality which lay behind Prout's statement is still
rife among a considerable majority of present-day musicians. It
is a conception which is based upon the tonality of classical music,
that is, a tonal organisation in which every note, every chord,
and every key-scheme stand in well-established and clearly defined
relations to a centre, the tonic. This organisation is based upon
the seven-note diatonic system with its two fundamental scales
and their twelve transpositions, the keys. The chief principle
upon which this whole organisation rests is the relationship of
the perfect fifth between notes, chords and keys. There is no

---

* I adopted this apt term from Sir George Dyson's *The New Music* (Oxford Press, 1924.)

doubt that the hierarchical order of classical tonality represents
the highest and at the same time the most organic form of tonal
organisation ever reached by Western music, and this for the
simple reason that the relationship of the fifth is the most natural
and closest—as the harmonic series proves. (So far as tonal
relationship is concerned the relationship of the perfect octave
is of no consequence.) But there are tonal organisations such
as the modal system or the complicated systems of Arabic and
Chinese music that are based upon principles of relationship
different from that of classical tonality. This very fact gives us
food for thought and will force us, as we shall see presently, to
reject Prout's statement which we take as representing the
general view. For if we were to accept it, the implication would
be that all Western music written before and after the period
from 1600 to 1890—to say nothing of Oriental and non-European
music in general—did not exist for us. It is clear that such a
view is untenable and stands in the way of a broader conception
of tonality. Nineteenth century musicians and scholars were far
too much wrapped up in classical tonality to perceive that it
represented only a very special form of possible tone-relations.
That the music based upon this form of tone-relations constitutes
one of the greatest periods in musical history should not blind
us to the fact that classical tonality has its limitations —limitations which musicians of the early romantic period had already
attempted to get rid of by expanding and enlarging the scope of
this tonality. And that this process of expansion gradually led
to a break-up of classical tonality and to novel forms of central
tone relations is *ipso facto* a proof that the natural laws underlying classical tonality have only limited validity. Thus the
classical conception of tonality seems to be of a similar relative
nature to that of the classical norm of dissonance. Just as the
norm of dissonance changed with different periods of musical
history so did the conception of what constituted tonal coherence
and central relations.

This argues a much broader conception of tonality than that in
which we were all brought up. In order to arrive at such a
conception we have to ask ourselves: what is the essential of
classical tonality? what is the general idea underlying it? We
all agree that, broadly speaking, it is the organising of our tone-
material in such a manner as to establish certain permanent
relations and functions between single notes, chords, and keys on
the one hand and a centre on the other. This centre consists
correspondingly of a single note (tonic note), a single triad (tonic
triad), and a single key (tonic key). If we take the mere existence
of certain permanent relations and functions of notes in respect of
a centre as the general idea of classical tonality, we are bound to
recognise that a similar idea underlies music that is not based on

classical tonality, Thus certain Oriental music and the music of the church modes have their form of tonality. And so, too, modern music—imagined by some to be a chaotic agglomeration of notes, chords, and lines—has *its* form of tonality in the sense that in a particular composition certain notes or sequences of notes, certain chords or chord progressions are given preference over others and thus establish temporary centres, which have a decisive bearing on the tonal organisation of the composition as a whole. In this light even "atonal" music, the music of the Schönberg school, has quasi-tonality which manifests itself in the permanent relationship between all the notes occurring in an "atonal" piece and the so-called tone-rows upon which it is based. (We shall discuss this problem in greater detail in the later part of the book, when also a brief outline will be given of Hindemith's attempt at establishing the tonality of modern music with the aid of his chromatic system.)

By accepting such a broader view it is necessary, however, that in speaking of tonality we should qualify it by adding whether we mean the tonal organisation of the modes, or the diatonic major-minor system, or the twelve-note music, or the Arabic *maquam*, or the Indian *raga*, or the Hebrew *weisen* or "modes"—all different kinds of extant tonal relationships.*

Just as the changes in the norm of dissonance influenced harmonic evolution so did the various forms in which tonal relations have been fixed. In other words, the vertical aspect of modal music is different from that of the diatonic major-minor system and this aspect is again different from that of whole-tone music or twelve-note music, and so on. The impression of that apparently chaotic state of modern music, of which the uninitiated so often complain, is partly due to the fact that these heterogeneous tonalities are frequently found side by side in modern works: modal elements and major-minor diatonicism; whole-tone, Oriental, and chromatic scales; chromatically intensified diatonicism and twelve-note music. And it is only natural that this mixture of tonal "styles" should have deeply affected the harmonic language of our days.

---

* Just before this book was going to press I came across Ernst Křenek's *Studies in Counterpoint* (G. Schirmer, Inc., New York, 1940), and was glad to see that Křenek arrived at the same conclusion of the need for a broader conception of tonality. Although he does not elaborate this point he makes it quite clear in the introduction to his book when he says that "it is undoubtedly possible to establish a broader definition of tonality. One might call tonality any method, of setting up recognisable relationships between musical elements. In this sense, the system of major and minor keys, characteristic of a certain historical period, would represent but one out of many conceivable aspects of tonality, and music that does not comply with the postulates of this system should show some other system of elementary relationships, *i.e.*, another type of tonality."

Thus we see how the three problems—the fixing of the norm of dissonance, the balance between horizontal and vertical polyphony, and tonality—have been operating in closest interaction to mould the physiognomy of modern harmony. The result of this composite process is thrown into a particularly sharp relief if we compare the following two examples between which lie nearly four centuries of harmonic evolution.

No. 3a. PALESTRINA, from the Nativity Motet, *Dies sanctificatus.*

No. 3b. SCHÖNBERG, *Klavierstück,* Op. 33a.

It is the chief aim of the following pages to disentangle the working of this process and to demonstrate in detail its effect upon harmony from about 1890 up to the present time.

PART II.

THE CHORD

I. Basic Structure: Chords of the Third and the Fourth

In our Western system of twelve semitones within the octave there are two basic principles of chord building: the super-imposition of thirds and fourths. All modern chords can be traced back to these two principles or their combination.

The following three examples illustrate the modern application of these two principles:

No. 4a. BARTÓK, *14 Bagatellen*, Op. 6, No. 4.

No. 4b. STRAVINSKY, *Le sacre du Printemps.*

No. 4c. VAUGHAN WILLIAMS, *On Wenlock Edge*, No. 5.

No. 4a: chords of piled-up thirds; No. 4b: chords of piled-up fourths; No. 4c: combination of thirds and fourths in one chord.

Let us for a moment consider the example from Bartók's *14 Bagatellen, Op. 6.* There are two points which call for special attention. The first is the harmonisation of an old Hungarian folk-song first with common triads and then with chords of the seventh and ninth; the second point is the non-resolution of these dissonant chords. What does Bartók imply by not resolving them? By this he obviously means to give the chords of the seventh and ninth the same status as that of the common triads. He stresses this intention by the juxtaposition of the two different harmonisations of the same tune. By the superimposition of further thirds the common triad is transformed into a dissonant chord that now assumes the role of the former. The general lesson to be drawn from this example is, that the dissonant chord in modern music frequently usurps the part of the triad. It has no preparation and no resolution. It has become completely independent and stands in its own right. This phenomenon is one of the many manifestations in which the modern feeling of the relative nature of the dissonance expresses itself.

The replacement of the common triad by chords of the seventh, ninth and so on has, however, come about gradually. It is a process the origin of which can be traced back to the treatment of the chord of the diminished seventh in classical music. This chord is, historically speaking, the first among all dissonant chords to remain without resolution. There are frequent examples in classical music, particularly in development sections and passages of a fantasia-like and improvisatory character, where whole chains of unresolved diminished sevenths occur with only the last chord resolving into a common triad (see Ex. No. 21a, from Mozart's Piano Concerto in C minor, K. 491, or *La Malinconia* from Beethoven's Op. 18, No. 6). With the romantic period the tendency to replace triads by chords of the seventh became more and more pronounced. Moreover, whereas the classical composers confined themselves on the whole to the use of dominant sevenths, diminished sevenths, and secondary sevenths on the supertonic, the romantic composers introduced chords of the seventh and, later on, of the ninth, eleventh, and so on, upon all the other degrees of the diatonic and chromatic scales. But all the same, they still felt the need to resolve them even though by very roundabout ways. A device that largely contributed to the modern substitution of triads by dissonant chords was the resolution of chords of the seventh, not into triads, but again into other dissonant chords as in the chains of diminished sevenths in classical music. The next step was chains of dominant sevenths as in Ex. No. 5a, or Ex. No. 5b, the latter showing a progression of five dominant sevenths intermingled with secondary sevenths.

No. 5a. SCHUMANN, Fantasiestücke, Op. 12 ("Ende vom Lied")

No. 5b. WAGNER, Siegfried (Act I).

No. 5c. MAHLER, Das Lied von der Erde ("Der Abschied")

No. 5d. STRAVINSKY, Sacre du Printemps.

It may, incidentally, be seen from these two examples how such chains of unresolved chords lead to the avoidance of melodic and harmonic caesurae, a fact which conforms exactly to the general tendency of romantic music to let the sounds flow into each other and thus cover up the joins. (French Impressionism shows this tendency in its most developed form.) If the music of the earlier romantic composers usually shows a predominance of the dominant seventh over secondary sevenths, with the late romantic and early modern schools, the position is almost reverse as illustrated by Example No. 5c with its chromatic side-slipping of secondary chords with major sevenths, of which only the last with the resolution of E flat on to D suggests a dominant seventh.* The same applies to secondary chords with more than three piled-up thirds such as secondary ninths, elevenths and thirteenths. And if the mollifying thirds are left out we arrive at the bare sevenths and ninths as shown in Example No. 5d. (The modern principle of consecutive dissonant intervals as exemplified in Nos. 5b, c, d, will be discussed in a later chapter.) The attraction of such passages lies in the very bareness of the intervals, a fact which also explains the extensive use made of bare perfect fifths. The early *organum*, the folksongs, and the music of primitive tribes are full of them, particularly in the form of drones. Its hollow sound and its bleak colour have made the bare fifth a perfect chord** to express sadness, melancholy, the eerie and the mystical. Typical examples of its use for such effects are the opening of Beethoven's Choral Symphony; the Dutchman's motif in Wagner's *The Flying Dutchman;* the opening of Wolf's *Die Geister am Mummelsee;* the opening of the third act of Puccini's *La Bohème.* (See Ex. No. 24a.)

As bare fifths frequently occur in primitive and early medieval church music, composers have used them also to express the elemental, the barbaric, the biblical, the pastoral, and the exotic. See, for instance, the bare fifths in Bartók's harmonisation of the old Hungarian folk-song (Example No. 4a); the piled-up bare fifths in Stravinsky's *Sacre du Printemps* (Example No. 6b); the "bitonal" fifths at the opening of the Shepherd's Hymn in Beethoven's Pastoral Symphony; the frequent passages of bare fifths in Vaughan William's ballet *Job* and in Puccini's *Turandot.* It is obvious why music that cultivates colour and sound for their own sakes, like French Impressionisms, should be particularly fond of bare fifths. (For details about the use of chords of

---

* This gradual ostracism of the dominant seventh may be accounted for by its clear and definite function in the major-minor system. We always expect it to lead to the tonic triad. With the expansion of tonality and the consequent loosening of strict and firm harmonic relations the dominant chord—next to the tonic triad the main pillar in our functional system—had to go by the board. (See page 43-47)

** Bare fifths are, strictly speaking, not true chords as the definition of a chord is the combination of at least three different notes. But as bare fifths may be interpreted as triads with the third left out, the designation "chord" is justifiable.

the seventh, ninth, and the bare consecutive fifths in French impressionistic music, see vol. I, chap. 1-3.)

It was said before that the superimposition of further thirds transforms the common triad into a dissonant chord. In other words, the common triad has been "spiced" and made more pungent. This is one of the chief reasons for the predominance of dissonant over consonant chords in modern music. Moreover, the superimposition of thirds also leads to a marked increase of the sound volume—an effect much sought after by modern composers. Thus we often get note-clusters as in the following examples :

No. 6a. BRUCKNER, 7th Symphony, 1st Movement.

No. 6b. STRAVINSKY, Le Sacre du Printemps.

No. 6c. MILHAUD, Cristophe Colomb. (No. 19.)

(see also Example No. 8b, or Liszt's Mephistowalzer: dominant fifteenth on E; Wolf, Lieder nach verschiedenen Dichtern, No. 10: dominant eleventh on C; Scriabin, Fifth Sonata, "Languido" section : dominant thirteenth on F sharp; Stravinsky, Petroushka, "Dance Russe": cadence with secondary and dominant elevenths.)

Let us now turn to the second principle of basic chord structure: the superimposition of perfect fourths.* To begin with, we have to ask ourselves whether the perfect fourth belongs to the consonances or the dissonances. There is no clear-cut answer to it and most probably there never will be one. The perfect fourth is a curious interval that has sworn allegiance to neither group. During nearly a thousand years it has continually changed its position from a consonance to a dissonance and vice-versa—incidentally one of the best proofs of the relative nature of the norms of consonance and dissonance. In the early stages of polyphonic music, the *organum* period, the perfect fourth was considered a consonant interval. Later on, as is evident from the old rules of strict counterpoint, it became a dissonance and was treated accordingly. To the classical composers it was a dissonance when its root formed the bass. In that case its upper note was considered an appoggiatura or suspension to the third as, for instance, in the cadential six-four chord which is not the second inversion of the tonic triad as often stated, but a double appoggiatura or suspension to the dominant chord. In all the cases, however, where the fourth was an inversion of the fifth as, in the chord of the sixth, it was treated as a consonant interval. Modern composers seem, on the whole, to regard the perfect fourth as a consonance, for they have raised it to the same status of a basic chord-building interval as the third of traditional harmony.

There are instances in classical and romantic music where certain chords look as if they were built up of fourths. But on closer examination they reveal themselves as specious fourth-chords resulting from appoggiaturas, passing-notes, and pedals. Thus, for instance, in bars 73-76 of Brahm's Rhapsody in E flat major, the combination of a pedal on C in the lower middle part with the dominant chord of C major produces a chord that differs in nothing but origin from the true fourth-chord of modern composers. (See also Beethoven's use of the perfect fourth F-B flat as a pedal at the conclusion of the last movement of the *Hammerklavier* Sonata, or Chopin's chords of the fourth produced by appoggiaturas, in bars 34-36 and later, of his Study Op. 10, No. 5.) Yet such and similar chord formations paved the way for the building of chords with the perfect fourth as basic interval. That romantic music already knew the special effect of the fourth, whether perfect or augmented, is shown by the tendency of some late-nineteenth century composers to throw this interval into relief by a special lay-out of the chord and thus make it

---

* Chords built up of augmented fourths are not possible in our tempered scale as the third note would be enharmonically identical with the upper octave of the first note. as, for instance, in the chord C-F sharp-B sharp (C).

stand out from the harmonic texture as in Example No. 7a, with its *organum*-like progressions of perfect fourths:

No. 7a. WOLF, *Auf ein altes Bild.*

No. 7b. STRAUSS, *Electra.*

No. 7c. STRAUSS, ibid.

No. 7d. STRAUSS, *Salomé.*

In Wolf's *Zur Warnung*, bars 3, 6, 8 and 10 of the piano accompaniment, the chord of the diminished sevenths is laid out in such a manner as to form two bare augmented fourths; L.H.: A flat-D; R.H.: F-B.   Strauss, in his *Elektra*, is particularly fond of the bare tritone and writes whole chains of it as in Example No. 7b.*

---

* It serves in this opera the purpose of expressing horror and morbid fear.   It may, incidentally, be remarked that the deliberate use of the augmented fourth occurs as early as the seventeenth century.   The harpsichord pieces of Giovanni Picchi, an Italian composer and organist, who lived at Venice round about 1620, are full of tritones. (See the article on that composer in Percy A. Scholes's *The Oxford Companion to Music*, Oxford University Press, 1938.)

The next example from the same work illustrates the combination of augmented and perfect fourths in one chord. But it must be emphasised that, in all these examples, it is the use of inversions of chords built up of thirds, and of their special lay-out which produces this specious form of fourth-chords. In contrast to this is Example No. 7d, the Prophet's motif, from Strauss's *Salomé*. Here the fourth C-F (bars 2-3) stands in its own right as an independent interval. It does not form part of a third-chord like the fourth G-C at the opening of the phrase nor is it the result of an appoggiatura like the tritone D sharp-A (bars 3-4). It is a stranger in this neighbourhood of tonal chords and, in fact, obscures for a moment the tonality of C major.

From this it is but a step to the genuine fourth-chord of modern music:

No. 8a. SCHÖNBERG, *Kammersymphonie*, Op. 9.

No. 8b. MILHAUD, *Cinq Symphonies*. No. I. 2nd Movement.

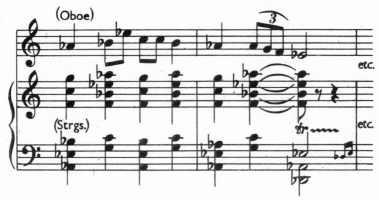

Example No. 8a shows in juxtaposition the double role of the

perfect fourth as a "generator" of melody and harmony.✻
Example No. 8*b* illustrates the comparatively rare instance of an
alternation of piled-up bare fifths and fourths as harmonization
of a tonal melody.

Schönberg, in his *Harmonielehre* (3rd edition, Vienna, 1921),
discusses the possibility of piling up so many perfect fourths
until one arrives at a chord which contains all the twelve notes
of the chromatic scale. With such a "synthetic" chord as basis
of a chromatic tone-system it would be possible to explain all
modern chord-combinations.

A similar idea seems to have been behind Scriabin's fourth-
chords which constitute an essential characteristic of his later
harmonic style.✻✻ Take, for instance, the so-called "mystic"
chord, the harmonic basis of his *Prometheus*:

No. 8*c*. SCRIABIN, *Prometheus*.

Scriabin arrives at this chord by adding to the major third C-E
four more thirds the notes of which he selects, not from the
diatonic scale, but the harmonic series. Thus he builds a chord
of the thirteenth, C-E (G)-B flat-D-F sharp A, but its individual
notes are so arranged as to suggest a chord built up of perfect
and augmented fourths.

Now Scriabin considered this formation a consonant chord and
treated it accordingly, upon the obviously wrong assumption
that, as it is built up of notes from the harmonic series like
the common triad, it consequently has the same status as the
triad—another example of the changed norm of consonance and

✻ The assumption is perhaps not quite unjustified that, like several other harmonic
innovations of modern music, the fourth was first used as a melodic step before it
became the basic interval of vertical combinations. Examples such as the Prophet's
fourths in Strauss's *Salome* or the opening theme of Schönberg's *Kammersymphony* with
its melodic progression of fourths seem to point in this direction. Somewhat akin to
this is the planning of a modulatory scheme in which the successive keys stand a perfect
fourth apart from each other, and I was quite surprised to find such an instance in
Johann Strauss's *Morgenblätter* in which the keys of the separate waltzes form a succession
of rising perfect fourths, i.e. G-C-F-B flat-E flat.

✻✻/As Gerald Abraham (*This Modern Stuff*, 2nd edition, Duckworth, 1939) points out,
Scriabin showed a predilection for the fourth already in his very early works.

dissonance in modern music. This chord is also called "synthetic" because it contains all four kinds of triads — major, minor, diminished and augmented. Thus it became for its inventor a harmonic reservoir which provided him with all sorts of chord-combinations. It was this quality that suggested to the composer the idea of making this chord the sole harmonic basis of a whole work. Yet the strangeness and beautifully iridescent colour of this and similar chords cannot make up for the almost complete loss of harmonic movement to which Scriabin's method inevitably leads. It is for this reason that many of his later works that are based upon such synthetic chords, are harmonically stagnant and monotonous.

One word on the use of mixed third- and fourth-chords. That we should find the two basic principles of modern chord-building in simultaneous combination is only natural. For modern music has, as I remarked before, invested the fourth-chord with the same powers and rights as the traditional third-chord. Thus, in Example No. 4c from Vaughan William's impressionistic song - cycle *On Wenlock Edge*, the chord of the thirteenth consisting of five piled - up thirds, forms a background of soft and blurred colour against which the hard and clear line of the bare fourths stands out all the more effectively. In the example below we witness how the fourth-chord, D-G-C-F-B flat, gradually comes into being and combines with the bare fifth, C sharp-G sharp,—the pedal of the first three bars. In the fourth bar, however, this hybrid chord resolves into a dominant ninth (plus added sixth) of E major thus leading back to a traditional chord formation.

No. 9. HONEGGER, *Le Roi David*. No. 16.

II. Chromatic Alteration

So far we have merely considered the basic structure of chords. Harmony, however, knows two means with which to embellish and, as often as not, complicate it: the chromatic alteration and the unessential note. The chords thus arrived at are not new chords in the strict sense but only derivations or functions of the basic forms. It lies in the nature of chromatically altered and unessential notes to produce dissonance and thus heighten and intensify the colour of the fundamental chords. They make the consonant chord more pungent, more "spicy". Dissonance creates harmonic tension, and as music, ever since the romantic period, has striven after an increase of tension, it becomes evident why chromatic alterations and unessential notes play such an important part in the evolution of modern harmony.

Let us first consider the chromatic alterations. I have already remarked that they owe their origin chiefly to the desire for increased dissonance and thus stronger harmonic tension. There is yet another additional cause and this is the need which our Western ear feels for the *subsemitonium modi* or leading-note. Take, for instance, the church modes in which a last residue of Oriental melodic feeling is still present. Of the six modes, four have no leading-note on the seventh degree. It was the need for the *subsemitonium*, gradually asserting itself that was responsible for the introduction into the modes of chromatic semitones between the seventh and eighth notes and for the sharpening and flattening of certain other notes. These chromatic alterations were not shown in the notation—hence the name *musica ficta* ('feigned music')—but were left to the medieval performers to sing or play them. This practice gradually led to the breakdown of the modal system in the sixteenth century and to the eventual establishment of our major-minor scales with their characteristic thirds and their leading notes on the seventh degree. Generally speaking, chromatic alterations create artificial leading-notes, a process which allows, melodically, a more fluent, pliable and supple part-writing, and, harmonically, a closer linking-up of the chords.

It is a historical fact that chromatic sharpening of a diatonic note occurs earlier in the evolution of music and is, on the whole, used to a wider extent than chromatic flattening. This may be accounted for by what one is inclined to call 'musical gravitation'. For the step-wise motion of notes down the scale seems to proceed with more ease and less amount of tonal energy than the motion upwards.* Chromatic flattening only increases this natural pull, whereas chromatic sharpening, by forcing the diatonic note to move upwards, appears to counteract the force of tonal gravitation. Nevertheless, there are already in early classical music typical instances of chromatic flattening, such as the flattened sixth in major resulting harmonically in the minor form of the subdominant; or the flattened second in minor—most likely to have originated in the desire to imitate the semitonal step from the tonic to the second degree of the Phrygian mode—which led to the chord of the Neapolitan sixth. One of the earliest examples of chromatic sharpening within the major-minor system, was the raised fourth degree, producing an artificial leading-note to the dominant. This was only natural as the dominant is next to the tonic the most important note of our tonal system, and it was therefore given its own leading-note. The harmonic result was a supertonic chord with a major third which took on the function of a dominant to the dominant, or *Wechseldominante* as the Germans call it. I mention this well-known phenomenon because out of it grew the *Zwischendominanten* or interdominants** which play such an important part in romantic harmony. They are an extension of the *Wechseldominante* technique, leading notes being formed to other degrees of the diatonic scale by chromatic alterations. Any chord that contains such an artificially created leading-note thus assumes the role of a dominant. This explains why the interdominants became an excellent means for abrupt transitions and modulations not only to related, but also to most remote keys as the next example shows:

No. 10. REGER, *Aus meinem Tagebuch*. Vol. 2. No. 8.

etc.

---

* This would also explain the relative frequency of suspensions and appoggiaturas resolving downwards.

** The English term has as far as I am aware been first used by Gerald Abraham in his *Chopin's Musical Style* (Oxford University Press, 1939).

The quick shift from the chord of C major to that of F sharp major is effected by one intervening chord: the diminished seventh on E sharp, arrived at by chromatic alteration and forming in its root the leading-note to the following F sharp major chord. It thus assumes the function of a temporary dominant to a completely unrelated key. It is clear from this simple example how the interdominants may be used not only for quite unexpected extensions of the original key, but for the loosening of tonal coherence and the eventual breaking-up of tonality. About this more will be said in a later chapter.

The increased desire for artificial leading-notes often results in simultaneous chromatic sharpening and flattening of the same diatonic note. The note is split into two semitones that pull in opposite directions as in the following examples :

No. 11a. SCHÖNBERG, Kammersymphonie, Op. 9.

No. 11b. BARTÓK, 14 Bagatellen. Op. 6. No. 10.

In the first example the note G, the fifth of the dominant seventh of F major, is split into G flat and G sharp (written as A flat in the first bar), which lead into F and A, respectively. Example 11b illustrates a progression of dominant ninths with simultaneous chromatic sharpening and flattening of their fifths. But in contrast to the Schönberg example, here the new leading notes are not resolved. The chromatic alteration "freezes" Its original purpose—to propel the movement of the diatonic note—is thus discarded.

And something else emerges from this example.   It is the fact that in modern music chromatically altered chords are treated in the same way as concords.   They are no longer considered as dissonant and consequently need no resolution.   They are used, as the Bartók example shows, as though they were consonant triads—again another manifestation of the modern view of the relativity of dissonance and consonance.

III. The Unessential Note

Unessential notes—suspensions, appoggiaturas, anticipations, pedals, passing and changing notes—serve, like the chromatic alterations, the general purpose of embellishing and enlivening the melodic line and the harmonic texture.   This the classics did chiefly on a diatonic basis.   Romantic and modern composers, however, have, with their greater sensibility to matters of sound and tone-colour, come to prefer the unessential notes of chromatic origin.   Just as they "spice" the chord by chromatic alterations, so they "ginger up" the melody with "foreign" chromatic notes.   In addition, the use of chromatic unessential notes, particularly of passing and changing notes, imparts to the melodic line a greater fluency, suppleness and plasticity than it is possible on a diatonic basis.＊

Unessential notes, whether diatonic or chromatic, are all dissonances according to traditional text-book harmony: But the changed feeling of modern musicians for the dissonance has affected the unessential notes, too, in that they are now being treated in a very free manner.＊＊

Let us for a moment recall the old text-book rules for the treatment of the unessential notes.   The first rule is preparation; the second, avoidance of their sounding together with the "true" note; and the third, resolution into a consonance.   How does

---

＊ How insipid a typically romantic melody becomes if its constituent chromatic notes are left out may be seen from a diatonic version of the "Tristan" motif:

No. 12. WAGNER, Tristan.

etc.

＊＊ Edwin von der Nüll (*Moderne Harmonik*, Leipzig, 1932) reports Bartók as saying that ever since his *14 Bagatellen Op. 6* he tried to employ the non-diatonic notes (meaning the chromatic unessential notes) as freely as possible.

this compare with the modern treatment? We need not concern ourselves with offences against the first rule, as already classical music furnishes us with countless examples of the unprepared entry of unessential notes. The only difference lies in the greater frequency with which this occurs in romantic and modern music. Also the second rule—avoidance of the clash with the " true " note—was broken by the classics as often as not, but usually when the " true " note formed the bass of the chord. The underlying idea was that if the rule was to be broken, unessential and " true " notes should be apart from each other as far as possible so as to smooth the harshness of the resulting clash. (The part which special spacing and scoring plays in this respect will be considered in a later chapter.) Romantic music gradually did away with this cautious procedure by putting the " true " note frequently in middle parts. But on the whole, it observed the rule that if unessential and " true " notes were to be sounded together they should never be at as close a distance as a second. In its tendency to increase both the degree and the number of dissonances, music from about 1890 onwards not only placed unessential notes and their resolutions very close to each other, but it also tended to accumulate several of such hard clashes in one single chord. It is from note-clusters such as shown in Example No. 13a, that the modern technique of unessential notes seems to have taken a hint:

No. 13a. BEETHOVEN, Choral Symphony. Finale

No. 13b. BARTÓK, 20 Hungarische Volkslieder. Vol. 2. No. 6.

No. 13c. BARTÓK, *14 Bagatellen.* Op. 6. No. 8.

etc.

Beethoven's four appoggiaturas, C sharp, E, G, and B flat, are sounded together with their notes of resolution resulting in a stridently dissonant chord—a chord which, incidentally, contains all the notes of the harmonic D minor scale.   Example No. 13b shows a similar simultaneous combination of several appoggiaturas with their "true" notes, the significant difference with the previous example being the chromatic nature of its unessential notes. Another symptomatic fact is that Beethoven resolves the dissonance almost at once, whereas Bartók, a century later, soaks himself in it for nearly six bars before resolving it.

A further complication of this method is, moving the resolutions on to other notes before the appoggiaturas have been resolved, as in Example No. 13c.   Here the sixths in the upper stave are appoggiaturas to the sixth in the lower.   But before they are resolved their "true" notes have moved a semitone down.   The result is a chromatic progression of two groups of consecutive sixths moving a minor ninth apart.   It conforms entirely to the modern treatment of the dissonance if, by this method, the resolutions into consonant chords are constantly postponed and the true relations between the unessential and their "true" notes obscured. * (See also Example No. 5c.)

From this it is but a step to the omission of the resolutions altogether.   The third text-book rule — the resolution of unessential notes—has no longer any validity for the modern composer.   It was the only rule that romantic music up to 1890, despite its great freedom otherwise, did observe.   The resolution of unessential notes was then either found in the next few bars or was transferred to another part.   The chief thing was that the resolution had to come sooner or later.   The exceptions that occur only confirm this general rule.   Yet it was only natural

---

* The beginnings of this process are already noticeable in romantic harmony when the bass moves away to another note before the resolution is completed.   The works of Schumann, Chopin, Liszt, Wagner, Wolf, and Brahms are full of such examples.

that with the changed feeling towards dissonance modern musicians should also dispense with the resolution of unessential notes altogether. Thus unresolved suspensions and appoggiaturas lead to most dissonant chords which stand now in their own right; passing notes quit their course freely by leaping either from or into a dissonant interval; and pedals are introduced and left off on dissonant notes. We shall presently see how some of these phenomena opened the way to the splitting of tonality and thus to bitonality and polytonality.

Here are a few examples to illustrate the various points made above:

No. 14a. SCHÖNBERG, *Buch der Hängenden Gärten* No. 10.

No. 14b. BARTÓK, *14 Bagatellen.* Op. 6. No. 6.

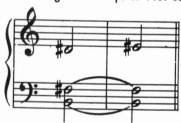

No. 14c. STRAUSS, *Also sprach Zarathustra.*

In Schönberg's cadence the tonic chord on G appears in the form of a dominant seventh with two unresolved suspensions, E flat and A sharp. It is the final chord of this song and plays here the same rôle as the tonic triad of classical and romantic music. Similarly, in the next example from Bartók's *14 Bagatellen, Op. 6*, the changing note E sharp does not return to its origin, D sharp. One of the most famous examples of unresolved appoggiaturas remaining in the air and producing the feeling of bitonality, is the end of Strauss's *Also Sprach Zarathustra*. The fact that the unresolved note C lies in the bass and has the last word, is mainly responsible for the impression of a clash between two different tonalities, B major and C major (Example No. 14c).

The following examples show other possibilities of the com·pletely free treatment of changing and passing notes :

No. 15a. STRAUSS, *Salomé.*

No. 15b. HINDEMITH, Das *Marienleben.* ("Geburt Christi.")

In the Salomé motif, the dissonant changing note A does not resolve into G sharp but leaps to another dissonant changing note, F double sharp, which in its turn is freely resolved into C sharp. In the Hindemith example, we expect the changing note D of the bass line (bar I) to return to C. Instead, it leaps to the dissonant G which finds its deferred resolution in the F sharp. The notes G and C of the second bar can be interpreted either as the lower unresolved changing notes of G sharp and C sharp, respectively, or as their chromatic flattening. However, the effect of this free treatment is a momentary feeling of bitonality—the clash of the two tonalities C sharp major- and C major-minor.

I have spoken before of the modern principle of sounding together the "true" note with its neighbouring or changing note. The constant application of this method is one of the most characteristic features of modern harmony and has led to the so-called "added note" chords. Its aim is, on the one hand, to "spice" the chords with seconds, particularly sharp dissonances; on the other, to thicken out the single note and thus increase the volume of sound. Again, this is only a modern application of an older principle, the thickening-out of melodic lines with thirds and sixths in classical and romantic music. The significant difference lies in the deliberate choice by modern composers of dissonant intervals.

Early examples of the modern "added note" chords are the triads with added sixths in late romantic music, particularly in cadences, as seen in the next two examples:

No. 16a. MAHLER, Das Lied von der Ede (" Der Abschied ").

No. 16b. DELIUS, Songs of Sunset.

The soft and blurred sound of these chords chiefly accounts for their frequent use in impressionistic music of a predominantly atmospheric character. *

---

* Some musicians trace the origin of these chords to the first inversion of the secondary seventh on the supertonic. More plausible, however, seems its derivation from a chord in which the passing note is sounded together with its note of origin:

No. 17

The following examples are typical of chord formations with one, two, and more neighbouring notes added to the fundamental structure:

No. 18a. STRAVINSKY, *Petroushka.*

No. 18b. BARTÓK, *Herzog Blaubarts Schloss.*

No. 18c. STRAVINSKY, *L'Oiseau de Feu.*

No. 18d. HINDEMITH, *Das Marienleben.* ("Vom Tode Mariä.")

No. 18e. STRAUSS, *Don Quixote.* Var. No. 2.

No. 18f. BERG, *Wozzek* (Act 3).

This device frequently leads to note-clusters and chordal monstrosities such as those in Examples Nos. 18e and 18f.* Example 18d illustrates again how the sounding together of the "true" chord with its neighbouring-note chord produces an apparent clash of two different tonalities (B flat-C)

We saw from some of the previous examples how the neighbouring note or chord may be brought into such close contact with the "true" note or chord that the resulting combinations are regarded only as the thickening-out of the fundamental structure. From this it is but a step to the complete replacement of the "true" note or chord by its neighbour. To use a metaphor, the deputy takes over the place of his chief and assumes all his functions. Here are two examples of such " deputising " neighbour-notes or chords :

No. 19a. STRAUSS, Salomé.

No. 19b. SCHÖNBERG, Kammersymphonie. Op. 9.

---

* In both these examples it is an extra-musical idea that is responsible for the choice of such strange chords. In the first it is the illustration of Don Quixote's battle, in the second example, the exclamation "murderer" in the voice-part. Similarly, in Berlioz's *Symphonic Fantastique*, at the end of the third movement, the 'Scene aux Champs', the composer depicts the distant rumbling of thunder by drum rolls on the notes A flat-B flat-C-F, a strange chord which reveals itself as the first inversion of the F minor triad plus B flat as "added" note.

In Example No. 19a the bass part of the dominant ninth of C sharp major (marked by X) is replaced by its neighbouring chord a semitone higher, resulting in a violently dissonant clash with the chord in the treble, the latter representing part of the original dominant ninth, G sharp-B sharp-D sharp-F sharp-A sharp. The chord on A entirely assumes the function of the dominant chord proper and accordingly resolves into the tonic triad on C sharp. Similarly, in the Schönberg example the dominant of E major, B-F sharp, is replaced by its neighbouring notes a semitone lower, B flat-F. These two examples are sufficient to show how this technique of " deputising " notes or chords splits the original key and obscures tonal relationships.

IV. Chord Progressions

So far we have examined the chord as such, that is, it's fundamental structure and the modifications this structure undergoes by the modern application of chromatic alterations and unessential notes. The next question is : what are the relations of the chord to its fellow chords in modern music? Or, more precisely, what are the modern principles of chord progressions? The answer has two aspects. The first is the relation of chords between themselves without special reference to their tonal functions. This relation may best be studied in the way chords progress from one to another. The second is the tonal functions of the chords, in other words, their relationship to a tonal centre. This relationship—tonality in the wider sense—will be discussed in the third part of this book.

The movement of chords in classical music was chiefly determined by cadential steps, the underlying formula of such progressions being I(-IV)-V-I or some elaboration of it with the aid of the other degrees of the diatonic scale. In this formula chromatic steps found their place, though it was only a limited one. All the same we find chromatic steps resulting in chromatic chord progressions as early as the end of the sixteenth century, the time when our chordal system was just in its chrysalis stage:

No. 20. Gesualdo da Venosa, from a Madrigal.

The Italian and English madrigalists, Purcell, Schütz, Bach and other composers of the older periods used chromaticism, both melodically and harmonically, in almost as bold a fashion as the late-romantic composers. In the music of the Viennese classical composers, however, with its iron-cast organisation of tonal functions, chromatic progressions became less frequent than in the previous period. For the chromatic step tends to loosen and momentarily obscure the strict harmonic logic upon which this music is based. Nevertheless, examples such as the following ones show conclusively that the great Viennese composers knew the special effects of chromatic progressions and sudden chromatic side-slippings :

No. 21a. MOZART, Piano Concerto in C minor, K491. 1st Movt.

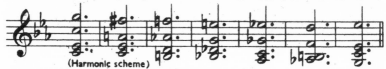

No. 21b. HAYDN, *The Creation*. Introduction.

No. 21c. BEETHOVEN, Piano Sonata, Op. 109. 2nd Movt.

It was only natural that in romantic music, with its higher emotional tension and its greater sensitiveness to tone-colour, chromatic chord progressions should gradually gain ascendancy over the diatonic ones.* The majority of such progressions originate in the harmonisation of chromatic passing notes in the treble or the bass. The resulting chords are purely transitional and have no independent function. They are merely the chordal links between two harmonic pivots as, for instance, in the famous example from Strauss's *Till Eulenspiegel* :

No. 22. STRAUSS, *Till Eulenspiegel.*

The "Eulenspiegel" motif appears here in the form of a melodic *ostinato* against which is set a bass line consisting of chromatic passing notes that move downwards and upwards. Each of these notes is harmonised, thus resulting in a progression of purely, transitional chords which form the bridge between the pivotal chords indicated by x. Were it not for the *ostinato* each single note of these transitional chords would show a strict semitonal

---

* Chromaticism seems to act as a ferment. It is significant that pronounced chromaticism only appeared in the embryonic stage of classical harmony (see Ex. No. 20) and again at the end of the nineteenth century when classical harmony began to undergo radical changes and to disintegrate.

movement.   In the next example there are two lines of chromatic
passing notes in contrary motion, of which the one in the bass
is harmonised with transitional chords of the fourth.   As in the
Strauss example, these chords are but the link between two
harmonic pivots.

No. 23.   SCHÖNBERG, *Buch der Hängenden Gärten*.   No. 3.

In passing, it may be remarked that the harmonisation of
passing notes tends to destroy their true character.   The fact
that each passing note is given its own separate chord lends it
far greater harmonic importance than is its due.   The chief
reason why this method became so characteristic of late nineteenth and early twentieth-century harmony is apparently that it
heightens the colour of the harmonic texture and at the same
time increases the volume of sound—both typical tendencies in
the harmonic style from 1890 onwards.   The classical composers
with their ideal of economy in colour and sound volume, as a rule,
left passing notes completely unharmonized or added to them
only a few occasional notes in two-part harmony.   They rarely
resorted to whole blocks of chords and thus preserved the
intrinsic nature of the passing notes.

Let us return to the Schönberg example (No. 23).   It illustrates
another seemingly modern device: the parallel motion or side-
slipping of the same chord resulting in a stream of chordal blocks.
Again, this is only a modern application of a very ancient device
that is known under the name of fauxbourdon—the parallel
motion of sixth chords in early polyphonic music.   The side-
slipping of chords is possible on a chromatic, diatonic or whole-
tone basis.   If in the second case—diatonic side-slipping—the
intervals of the chords are not altered by accidentals demanded
by the given key, the tonal coherence is at once broken.*   This

---

* In a way this resembles the "real" answer as against the "tonal" in a fugue with a
modulating subject.

rigid method is most favoured by modern musicians. The
following examples illustrate some possibilities of side-slipped
intervals and chords: parallel bare perfect fifths (a): parallel
perfect fifths 'thickened-out' with added seconds (b): parallel
fourths chords (c): parallel augmented triads on a whole-tone
basis (d): parallel chords of the seventh and ninth (e). (For
parallel bare sevenths and ninths, see example No. 5d).

No. 24a. PUCCINI, La Bohème (Act 3)

No. 24b. BARTÒK, 14 Bagatellen. Op. 6, No. 5.

No. 24c. Ibid. No. 9.

No. 24d. SCHÖNBERG, Kammersymphonie. Op. 9.

No. 24e. STRAVINSKY, Petroushka.

These examples also show another modern device: the 'thickening-out' of a single-line melody by chordal blocks. This is nothing else but an extension of the "added-note" technique which we discussed in the previous chapter. Again, these streams of chords have no tonal function but only serve the purpose of heightening the harmonic colour and increasing the sound volume. We shall see in a later chapter how such chordal streams can be contrapuntally combined in the same way as single-line melodies are set against each other.

Somewhat akin to the side-slipping of chords are parallel progressions by intervals bigger than a second as, for instance, in the following example or in Example No. 11b, with the roots of the seventh- and ninth-chords moving by thirds.

No. 25. SCRIABIN, 5th Piano Sonata.

These two examples are only more modern illustrations of the *Terzrückung*, as the Germans call it, or mediant key relationship— so characteristic of romantic harmony.* Like the chromatic, the mediant progressions were one of the first harmonic means to break, or at any rate obscure, the clear functional organisation of keys in classical music. It was the sudden and abrupt change of key and, consequently, of colour that made the mediant progressions a frequent device in romantic harmony. They often replace the circle of fifths of classical music by a circle of thirds** as in the example from a Liszt song:

No. 26a. LISZT, *Wandrers Nachtlied.*

---

* Occasional instances of it are to be found as early as the second half of the eighteenth century.

** Among twentieth-century composers, Reger was particularly fond of the mediant chord progression. Influenced by Riemann's *Funktionstheorie* he went so far as to

Here are some more recent examples of mediant chord progressions :

No. 26b. STRAUSS, *Elektra.*

No. 26c. VAUGHAN WILLIAMS, *Job.* 1st Scene.

No. 26d. WALTON, *Belshazzar's Feast.*

Another progression much favoured by modern composers is that by an augmented fourth—perhaps the most powerful means of breaking tonal coherence by the simple juxtaposition of completely unrelated chords. It is for this reason that the *diabolus in musica,* as medieval theorists significantly called the

---

substitute the dominant and the subdominant—sometimes even the tonic — by their respective mediant chords, viz. common triads on C-E flat-C or C-A flat-E flat-C which stand for the ordinary cadences C-G-C or C♯-F-G-C respectively. (See Reger, *Modulationslehre,* Leipzig, 1904.

augmented fourth, has been used by modern composers as dynamite with which to blow up the citadel of classical tonality. Here are a few examples :

No. 27a. STRAUSS, *Elektra.*

No. 27b. ELGAR, *The Apostles.*

No. 27c. BARTÓK, *14 Bagatellen.* Op. 6, No. 13.

The *Bagatelle* from which the Bartók example is taken is actually based on the alternation of the E flat minor and A minor chords.✻

✻ It is interesting to see how Beethoven came very near the modern progressions by tritones. In the third movement of his *Hammerklavier* Sonata, Op. 106, there is a passage (bars 21 to 22 and the corresponding bars in the recapitulation) in which occurs a sudden shift from the tonic triad of C sharp major to that of G major, with only an intervening diminished seventh on C sharp to effect this unexpected transition.

In conclusion a few words on the elision—the omission of notes and chords which by long habit and tradition we have come to take for granted, or which, from the musical context, we expect to follow. In a way the elision can be compared to the telegraphic style in which obvious and matter-of-course words are obviated. In some works of modern literature as, for instance, in (parts of) James Joyce's *Ulysses*, we find a similar technique. The underlying idea is to avoid the obvious and the trite, to make the style more succinct and taut, and to introduce an element of surprise.

For obvious reasons, harmonic elisions will be most effective in certain well-worn formulae and formula-like progressions such as cadences. One of the earliest examples of a cadential elision is the omission of the six-four chord between the chord of the Neapolitan sixth—by its nature a chromatic passing-note chord—and the dominant as shown in Example No. 28a:

No. 28a.

No. 28b. CHOPIN, Study, Op. 25. No. 1.

No. 28c. STRAUSS, *Ein Heldenleben.*

In Example No. 28b it is the obvious dominant of A flat major—the resolution of the six-four chord suspension—that is taken for granted and consequently left out. In the third example the elision is effected by the unexpected replacement of the tonic E major by its neighbouring chord E flat major. If Wagner, at the beginning of the Tristan Prelude, omits the triads of A minor, C major and E major, which we expect to follow their respective dominants, it is at bottom the same as when modern composers do not bother about the obvious resolution of dissonances. In fact, quite a number of examples that I have quoted in connection with the free treatment of unessential notes could also be accounted for by the principle of elision.

PART III.

TONALITY

I. Expansion and Break-Up of Classical Tonality

I remarked in a previous chapter that the fact that classical tonality was the basis of the music of one of our greatest periods in the history of music should not blind us to its limitations, limitations which successive generations of composers attempted to get rid of. This they did by expanding and enlarging the scope of classical tonality. Yet the logical course of this process inevitably led to a gradual break-up of this form of tonality and finally to its replacement by various novel orders of tonal relationship. How did all this come about?

The simplest and at the same time the clearest and most final form in which classical tonality expresses itself is the cadence I-V-I. Tonic and dominant—they are the pillars of classical tonality like the father and mother of the human family. For eighteenth-century music the relation between tonic and dominant was the chief basis of harmonization and modulation. It is for this reason that the music of this period—the acme of classical music—represents a model of clear and definite tonality. This does not mean that other degrees of the diatonic scale were not used. (There exists, it is true, some music of this period that employs only these basic harmonies.) But they were used with much less frequency than tonic and dominant, whether of the original key or that of a modulating section. In other words, the whole organisation of classical tonality was founded upon the relation of scalar degrees, chords, and keys that are a perfect fifth away from each other. The degree of this relationship was determined by the distance in which chords and keys stood in the circle of fifths. The nearer this distance was from a given starting point—the tonic—the closer was the relationship. The circle of fifths extends from the starting point in two directions, in rising and falling fifths. Yet of the two, the circle of rising fifths has, by virtue of the importance of the rising fifth in the harmonic series, pride of place. This, incidentally, partly explains why the sub-dominant—the degree a fifth down from the tonic—is relatively less important than the dominant.

It was through this circle of fifths—the symbol of tonal hierarchy in classical music—that the tonic exercised its influence, direct and indirect. Through it the tonic dominated the whole harmonic and, consequently, formal structure of classical music, beginning with the simple cadence through the short four- and eight-bar periods up to entire sections and movements. Even the key-relationship between the four movements of the sonata form was based upon the circle of fifths, with the tonic key of the first movement as the centre. The form of the suite— historically older than that of the sonata—showed an even more autocratic regime of the tonic in that as a rule all the movements were in the key of the first movement.

It was against this tyranny of the tonic and its strong executive power, the circle of fifths, that the romantic composers began to rebel. The strict logic of the tonal relationships in classical music no longer corresponded to romantic ideals. The higher degree of emotionalism, the influence of poetical and literary elements, the gradually developing sense for tone-colour for its own sake resulting in greater stress being laid on the more sensual aspect of music, the dislike of sharp outlines and distinct contours, the tendency to blur the sounds and allow them to flow into each other ; all this and more combined to undermine the autocratic hierarchy of classical tonality.

The general aim of the romantic composers was gradually to curtail the all-pervading influence of the tonic and eventually remove it from its dominating position. To this end various means were applied. Other degrees of the diatonic scale besides the first (tonic), fourth (sub-dominant), and fifth (dominant) were used with increasing frequency. The common triad—the symbol of classical tonality—gave way to dissonant forms such as chords of the seventh, ninth, and so on. The technique of the unessential notes was intensified with the avowed aim of obscuring tonal relations. The romantics did not break the backbone of classical tonality. That was left to some modern composers of the extreme school. But they were able to deal the circle of fifths a severe blow by setting up against it tonal relations that are based on chromatic and mediant steps. Instead of using the diatonic degrees of the scale they showed a marked preference for the chromatic forms. Chromaticism permeated not only melodic lines but also chords, and chord progressions. And it greatly influenced the key-scheme of modulations. In contrast to the gradual and comparatively slow and steady transitions from one key to another characteristic of the mainly diatonic modulations of the classics, chromaticism permitted a quick, sudden, and unexpected change of keys. Chromatic alteration interdominants, enharmonic changes, and chord progressions by semitones, thirds, and augmented fourths, were all pressed into service in order to quit the tonic chord or key as quickly and suddenly as possible and to rush from one key to another.* The chromatic progressions and modulations of romantic music, particularly of the later period, are often like zig-zag journeys across most beautiful country, yet journeys that are made for their own sake rather than to reach a certain point.

Chromatic harmony was chiefly responsible for the expansion and the enrichment of classical tonality Take any work by Schubert, Schumann, Chopin, Brahms, Wolf, or Wagner, and compare its chord formations, chord progressions, and key-schemes with those of classical compositions : you will see at a glance how much richer romantic harmony is and how much wider the orbit of tonality becomes. In point of fact, one of the chief technical characteristics of romantic music in general, is the development of the harmonic language, chiefly with the aid of chromaticism, into an ever-ready and most supple means by which to express the typical feelings and thoughts of the romantic artist. The romantic period in music was the Golden Age of harmony.

But it lay in the nature of this process of continual expansion and enrichment that it eventually led to a weakening and loosening of the central power—the tonic—by which classical melody and harmony were held together. The tonic was gradually pushed into the background : the tonic triad appeared with diminishing frequency until it scarcely occurred at all in the course of a piece; and the tonic key was quitted immediately after it had been established, to be followed by sudden harmonic shifts and modulations which led sometimes to keys very distantly or not at all related to the tonic. Good examples of this gradual eclipse of the tonic are, for instance, Chopin's *Prelude*, Op. 28, No. 2, in A minor, Loewe's ballad *Archibald Douglas*, and Wagner's Prelude to *Tristan*. In these works the tonic hardly appears but it is hinted at by chords and keys that by their context reveal themselves as related to the tonic thus circumscribing it. If in these and other similar examples of romantic music the feeling of tonality is not so strong as it was in classical works, we have all the same no doubts as to the central key which directs the harmonic course from " behind the scene " and holds the piece together. But the nearer we come to the end of the nineteenth and the beginning of the twentieth centuries, the more difficult

---

* Beginnings of this process are already noticeable in classical music, notably in two Instances : the " real " sequence with its disregard of the tonic key, and the chromatic side-slipping of diminished seventh. But there is a world of difference between the occasional and casual use of certain devices and their constant and permanent application.

it becomes to relate chords and keys to a tonic centre. Take, for instance, the very beginning of Strauss's *Salomé*, an epitome of Strauss's general harmonic style. Its tonic key, C sharp minor, disappears completely after the third bar and a continual modulatory "chase" begins that leads with kaleidoscopic rapidity through various other keys To make the tonal relations more obscure still, the temporary tonic triads of these keys do not appear themselves, but are replaced by their dominants or transformed into chords of the seventh with appoggiaturas and passing notes into the bargain. This example, to which innumerable other examples from works written during 1890-1910 could be added, shows classical tonality in the process of complete disintegration.

Now what are the principles by which harmony of this period is governed? Chief of them is the principle of sound and colour for their own sakes. These two elements—purely sensual and irrational—begin to determine the choice of chords and chord progressions, and gradually gain ascendancy over the rational element of classical harmony, *i.e.* the necessity to relate every chord, every chord progression and every key to a tonal centre and to make them a function of it. This tendency fully developed in the music of the French Impressionists (see Vol. I.)

Another principle is to allow special contrapuntal and thematic designs to dictate the harmonic course and we shall presently see to what results its rigid application may lead.

Last but by no means least mention must be made of the influence of literary and programmatic ideas. It is no mere coincidence that a number of harmonic novelties made their first appearance in the songs, operas, and symphonic poems of the romantic period. We know that poetic and dramatic ideas have often stimulated composers to find new and hitherto untried harmonic effects. (Tempting as it would be to show how much in the evolution of modern harmony was due to the influence of extra-musical ideas, it would go far beyond the scope of this book.)

I remarked before that it was the extreme school of modern composers who set themselves the task of breaking the backbone of classical tonality. This they did, first, by dispensing with the dominant. With this step they destroyed one of the strongest pillars of classical tonality. The tonic was thus deprived of its main assistant to assert its power. The tonic chords and keys no longer occupy the distinguished position of heretofore; they do not stand out from other chords or keys as they did in classical harmony, and hardly enjoy any special privileges. Something approaching musical communism has replaced the autocratic hierarchical system of classical tonality.

This is best shown by the endings of some modern works where, from the point of view of classical and romantic harmony, there is no cadence at all. Take, for instance, the cadence from Bartok's *Bagatelle, No. 13* (Example No. 27c.) The two chords on A and E flat, respectively, are to all intents and purposes of equal importance. Were it not for the fact that the piece opens and concludes with the second chord and uses it more often than the first there would be no other criterion for regarding it as the tonic harmony. There is no cadential chord progression, not a single dominant in the whole piece, to indicate the tonic function of the E flat minor harmony. (We know already from examples of romantic music that openings and endings are no longer safe criteria for determining the tonic.)

Yet Bartok's piece has its own kind of tonality, a tonality in the modern sense, *i.e.* some notes or chords gain, by the special way in which they are used, a certain importance and value that give them something approaching the function of a tonic. It is usually by the frequency of their appearance and their use at architecturally important points that such chords and chord progressions receive a certain distinction. It would be against the facts, however, to ascribe to them more than a very weak power of centralisation. The relation between such chords and others is from the point of view of classical tonality loose and casual, yet it does create a feeling of tonality if only of the vaguest kind. Take again Bartók's *14 Bagatellen, Op. 6*✻ and examine them from the point of view of tonality. It will be found that the "tonic" chords and chord progressions in the sense just described are: In No. 2, D-A flat-B flat; In No. 5, G-B flat-D-F; in No. 6, the major triad on B; in No. 7, the chord progressions of the first two bars; in No. 10, the major triad on C; in No. 11, the chord of the fourth G flat-C flat-E flat-A flat; and finally, in No. 13, the minor chord of the seventh on E flat.

II. The Splitting of Keys: Horizontal Methods, Bitonality and Polytonality, Heterophony

We have seen in the previous chapter how the enrichment and the gradual expansion of classical tonality eventually led to

---

✻ I think I owe the reader an explanation for my frequent quotations from this work. It is not only easily accessible to everybody and being a piano composition, easy to read, but I also consider it the best compendium of most devices of modern harmony.

its complete disintegration and practically to the abolition of a central governing power.   Instead of one dominating tonic every chord progression and every little passage seem now to have its own tonic centre, which has very little or no relation at all with the others.   It is, to use a metaphor, as if our planetary system (classical tonality) with the sun as its centre (tonic) had been destroyed by some elemental force: the planets (temporary tonics) are no longer ruled in their course by the sun but have become free and independent to establish, each for itself, a new centre.   The cosmos is split into microcosms.

One form of this splitting up of a central key has become a special feature of modern music, which is known as bitonality and polytonality—the dissolution of one key in two and more keys that run simultaneously on different tonal planes.   But this did not come about at once.   Bitonality has its historical forerunners: for instance, the fluctuation between two main keys.   This is what Schönberg in his *Harmonielehre* aptly calls *schwankende Tonalitat* ('fluctuating tonality ').   Take, for instance, the last movement of Beethoven's String Quartet, Op. 59, No. 2, with its wavering between the keys of C major and E minor, or Schumann's *Im schönen Monat Mai* which alternates between F sharp minor and A major.* More modern examples are, for instance, the Hero's theme in Strauss's *Ein Heldenleben* (E flat major-C minor) or Mahler's song-cycle *Lieder eines fahrenden Gesellen*: No. 1, D minor-G-minor; No. 2, D major-B major; No. 3, D minor-E flat minor; No. 4, E minor-F major-minor. These and similar other cases already show a kind of bitonality as the music centres round two different keys.   The difference with true bitonality lies in the fact that the two keys do not appear simultaneously.

Nearer to true bitonality comes the telescoping of major and minor triads into one single chord.   This simultaneous combination of the two diametrically opposed harmonic zones thus meeting at one point is an excellent means of obscuring tonality.   It obviously derived from the close succession of the major and minor forms of chords, as, for instance, at the opening of Strauss's *Also sprach Zarathustra* (C major-C minor), the beginning of the *Nachtmusik* in Mahler's Seventh Symphony (successive horn-calls in C major and C minor), and in the same composer's

---

* The modulation from minor to its relative major in the exposition of a movement in sonata form in a minor key may, to a certain extent, already be regarded as an example of fluctuating tonality.   And if we go back to the modal period, when our major-minor tonality was in the melting-pot, this fluctuation of "keys" becomes even more pronounced in the frequent alternation of a piece between the authentic and plagal forms of its particular mode.

Sixth Symphony, where the close alternation between the chords of A major and A minor attains the importance of a basic motif.* One of the earliest examples of a simultaneous mixture of major and minor occurs in Dargomizhsky's *Fantasia on Finnish Themes* (perf. 1869). But Western music took three to four decades before this device established itself. Here are a few examples of telescoped major and minor from more recent works: Mahler, Sixth Symphony, first movement; C major-C minor; Reger, *Böcklin Suite*, conclusion of the last movement: A major-A minor; Stravinsky, *Sacre du Printemps*, opening of the *Cercles Mysterieux des Adolescentes*: B major-B minor; Bliss, Viola Sonata, Coda: dominant seventh on A with a major and minor third; Walton, Viola Concerto, conclusion of the third movement: A major-A minor.

Another form of this simple and purely chordal bitonality is the telescoping of triads belonging to different keys, as, for instance, in the following example:

No. 29. STRAUSS, *Elektra.*

where the first chord consists of two piled-up triads of D flat major and B flat major, respectively. This chord is, however, laid out in such a way that the two different harmonic zones to which the triads belong are clearly marked. The example also shows how the chromatic side-slipping of this hybrid chord produces not only two harmonic streams but comes very near horizontal bitonality.

Now genuine bitonality and polytonality are frequently the result of modern horizontal writing and it will be interesting to study the means by which "multiple" tonality may be achieved.

---

* There is a historical precedent for this quick alternation between major and minor. It was a familiar device of the classical composers, particularly of Beethoven and Schubert, to repeat a motif or theme in its minor or major form, respectively, and thus create a sudden change of contrasting moods.

A first step in this direction lies in the rigid application of what may be generally called 'horizontal methods' by which classical tonality is obscured and even split. Contrapuntal devices such as the canon, the imitation, the combination of two or more themes, the consistent carrying through of melodic designs, and, generally, the play with motifs or whole themes lead, if rigidly applied, to tonal ambiguity and split tonality.* Such phenomena appear already in classical music. Thus in the following Bach example:

No. 30a. BACH, *Duetti for Clavichord or Harpsichord*

the canon a perfect fourth lower creates two different tonal planes: the upper part modulating from D minor to G minor, the lower from A minor to D minor. This is certainly bitonality. But there is one essential difference between this kind of bitonal writing and the modern variety. Bach, in contrast to most modern composers, is here as much concerned with the vertical factor as he is with the horizontal. See how careful he is to resolve the dissonant suspensions in the most "correct" manner. True, the tonality seems here dual but the logic of the part-writing and the treatment of the dissonances is such as to give this passage a clear tonal direction. Moreover, the resolution intervals imply triads and inversions that are closely related to D minor. In other words, vertically there is no tonal ambiguity at all. It is only if we consider this passage in its purely horizontal aspect that we gain the impression of dual tonality. It is just this very combination of clear vertical tonality and horizontal bitonality that constitutes the aesthetic attraction of this passage, a combination that is so often lacking in modern examples of bitonality and polytonality. Not even in his boldest contrapuntal writing does Bach forget to take the vertical factor

---

* Edwin Evans seems to go even farther when he says that "in spirit every canonic comes at an interval other than the octave and every fugal answer constituted tentatives towards bitonality." (See Article, *Atonality and Polytonality* in Cobbett's Cyclopedic Survey of Chamber Music, Oxford Press, 1929.)

into account, and this is perhaps the chief reason why his counterpoint is so much superior to the modern linear style.*

A good example in classical music of a split key caused by the
strict imitation of a motif is to be found in the first movement
of Beethoven's *Les Adieux* Sonata where toward its conclusion
tonic and dominant clash together in a strident dissonance. A
similar clash with the dominant is produced by the anticipation
of the tonic harmony in the famous passage which leads to the
recapitulation of the first movement of the *Eroica*. Nearer to
modern bitonality come the horn passages at the beginning of
the second act of *Tristan* with their combination of bare perfect
fifths on C and F over a pedal F. The contrapuntal combination
of three motifs, with little regard for the vertical result is shown
in the following example :

No. 30b, MAHLER, Das *Lied von der Erde* ("Von der Schönheit'')

---

* Modern musicians often seem to forget that the very life-blood of polyphonic music
is the inseparability of the horizontal and the vertical. This is what Sir Donald Tovey
presumably meant when he once said that "counterpoint is the statement of *harmony* in
the form of a combination of *melodies*."   (The italics are mine.)

It illustrates the very opposite of the Bach quotation. Here, the tonality of the three parts is clear as far as the horizontal aspect is concerned. It is a chromatically expanded C minor. Tonal ambiguity lies here only in the vertical aspect. Yet, like the Bach example, Mahler's passage must be considered in both its fundamental aspects, the horizontal *and* the vertical, in order to appreciate its full tonal import.

Another avenue of approach to bitonality lies in the modern treatment of the unessential note, particularly the sounding together of the "true" with their neighbouring-note chords, as may be seen from Examples Nos. 13a, b, c; 14c; 15b; 18d; 19a. In all these examples—and the reader will find innumerable others in most music written between 1890 and 1910—the unresolved unessential notes suggest the existence of another tonality, the tonality of the neighbouring key a major or minor second apart from the "true" note or chord. And finally there is the old device of pedals in the bass and inner parts—most certainly derived from the ancient drones—which contains already an element of bitonality, as Sir George Dyson pointed out. * If the pedal is horizontalised, that is to say, elaborated into a melodic line, which preserves the key against the harmonic changes in the other parts, we arrive at modern bitonality. (See the reference to Stravinsky's *Petroushka* on p. 56).

The following examples are typical of fully developed bitonality and polytonality. In the Ländler from Berg's *Wozzek* we encounter a bitonal cadence: E flat major in the two upper and G minor in the two lower staves.

No. 31. BERG, *Wozzek* (Act 2).

---

* The New Music (Oxford Press, London, 1924) and article "Harmony" in Grove's Dictionary of Music and Musicians. (London, 1940)

One of the most famous instances of bitonality—probably so because of its bare and therefore very telling form—is the simultaneous use of C major and F sharp major arpeggios in the compartment scene from Stravinsky's *Petroushka*. Another interesting example of modal bitonality is to be found in No. I of Bartók's *14 Bagatellen* : Aeolian on C sharp and Phrygian on C. Yet Bartók's part-writing is such as to produce consonant intervals on almost every strong beat of the bar. It is the peculiar musical orthography—four sharps in the treble and four flats in the bass—that makes this piece appear more dissonant than it actually sounds.

Polytonality—the combination of three and more different keys—is well illustrated in the next quotation :

No. 32. SZYMANOWSKI, String Quartet. Op. 37, 3rd Movement.

E minor triad ✳

Here we have the simultaneous use of C major, E flat major, F sharp major and A major—all keys a minor third apart from each other so that the four notes of a diminished seventh on C would represent the tonal scheme of this scherzo movement. In the ensuing trio this scheme is transposed a tone higher, which shows that modern composers often treat multiple tonality in the same simple way as the classics and romantics treated single keys. Milhaud, who at one time indulged in polytonal experiments, combines no fewer than five keys :

No. 33. MILHAUD, *Cinq Symphonies*. No. 4. Finale.

$$\left(\begin{array}{c}\text{A minor triad}\\\text{with appoggiaturas}\end{array}\right)$$

The movement from which I have taken the above passage is a ten-part fugue with two subjects. The first entry of the first subject is in F major and the four successive entries occur each a perfect fifth higher than the preceding one. In other words, the keys of the five entries are arranged in a circle of rising fifths, so that on the last entry we get a combination of the keys of F major, C major, G major, D major and A major. On reaching this climax, Milhaud complicates the contrapuntal texture by introducing his second subject in the top part.＊

Bitonality and polytonality are not restricted to the combination of single-line melodies. Following the modern tendency to employ several devices at the same time, composers have written polytonal passages in which the melodic lines are thickened-out into chordal streams (see p. 38), as, for instance, in the next example:

No. 34. VAUGHAN WILLIAMS, Pastoral Symphony, 1st Movement.

＊ These polytonal *tours de force* have their historical precedents. In certain works by an Italian composer, Pietro Raimondi (1786-1853), who performed the ingenious feat of writing three oratorios, each in a different key, which could be played simultaneously. Raimondi also wrote two symphonies and several four-part and six-part fugues which could be combined in the same manner (See Article *Pietro Raymondi* by Cecil Gray, *The Music Review*, London, February, 1940).

For curiosity's sake I also mention a little-known piece by Méhul (1763-1817), entitled *Ouverture Burlesque*, at the conclusion of which the composer introduces a *charivari* in which the tune appears simultaneously in the keys of C major, D major. B flat major, A major, and E major—the intention being to produce a ludicrously cacophonous effect which is the chief characteristic of these musical jokes. (See also Mozart's *Musical Joke*, K. 522, Rondo Finale.)

The modal top melody is thickened-out with octaves and perfect fifths against which is set a stream of six-four chords of 'E flattish' tonality. Milhaud, in the nineteenth tableau, Le Rédempteur, of his opera Christophe Colomb, has written this startling combination of chordal streams: orchestra, top part thickened-out by no less than seven piled-up thirds (see Example No. 6c), combined with blocks of common triads that move chromatically in contrary motion; chorus, the one section is given fauxbourdon-like progressions while the other sings a single-line melody in parallel octaves; and all this is built up on a complicated and independent instrumental ostinato in the bass part. In the opening scene of Stravinsky's Petroushka occurs the following passage: the Russian folk-tune is thickened-out into triads and first combined with a pedal-like chord of G minor. Then this chord is "horizontalised" into a melodic line which in its turn is thickened-out into a chordal stream, the whole resulting in a two-part bitonal counterpoint in which there are two different strands of triads and inversions instead of single-line parts. This example is, incidentally, a good illustration of the method, mentioned already on p. 52, to derive bitonality from extended pedals.

We have seen how some special applications of horizontal methods lead to multiple tonality. In this connection I have to mention a quasi-contrapuntal device of which some modern composers have availed themselves. This is what is known as heterophony. This term was first used by Plato to describe the only kind of horizontal polyphony that ancient Greek music knew. We still use it to-day to denote a similar kind of primitive counter-point to be found in Oriental and non-European music in general. Its principle consists in the simultaneous combination of a melody with its variations in other parts. But these variations never wander so far from the theme as to assume melodic independence. We think to hear different parts—a frequent experience in listening to Oriental music—but, at bottom, what we hear is always the same melody being incessantly varied in the other "parts." The following example from a Javanese "score" will make the principle of heterophony clear : *

No. 35a. Javanese " score."

* Quoted from Carl Stumpf, Sammelbände für vergleichende Musikwissenschaft, I.

The pentatonic "theme" lies in the lowest part. Though the other two parts seem to have melodies of their own, in fact, they merely play upon the pentachord D-F-G-A-C which is the tonal basis of the "theme." In other words, the two upper parts are variations or adumbrations of the melodic line A-G-F-G-F-D-C-D, the "theme" of the passage.

It was the growing contact which European musicians began to make with Oriental music and music of other non-European countries in the course of the second half of the nineteenth century that was responsible for the introduction of certain exoticisms into our Western art. One of them was heterophony, or, rather, a Western imitation of its basic principle, of which the next example taken from Puccini's *Turandot*, gives a fair illustration :

No. 35b. PUCCINI, *Turandot* (Act 3).

The trumpet part represents the "theme" and is based upon the anhemitonic (without semitones)—pentatonic tetrachord D-E-G-A. Oboes and clarinets play the "theme" in its vertical form, while violins and harp are given a motif that is derived from the inversion of the trumpet tune. And finally the flutes stress the chief notes of the tune, E and A, by playing them simultaneously in the form of perfect fifths and fourths, respectively. The three upper parts are consequently nothing else but a partly horizontal, partly vertical projection of the trumpet "theme" without any thematic independence. Similar heterophonic passages are to be found, for instance, in the opening scene of Stravinsky's *Petroushka*, and in his *Sacre du Printemps* between figures 28 and 30 of the miniature score, where the complex polyphony is as of the same nature as the Puccini example above.

So much for horizontal methods in modern music. But before we leave this subject, a few words must be said on the part that spacing and scoring play in producing the effect of modern counterpoint. Broadly speaking, there are two tendencies to be noticed. Modern composers try, on the one hand, to make the different contrapuntal strands stand out by wide spacing and contrasting instrumentation as in the example from Milhaud's *Christophe Colomb* (see p. 56), or Examples Nos. 34 and 35b. On the other, they seek to blur the outlines of the various parts and let them flow into each other by deliberate narrow spacing and similar or even identical scoring. This latter technique is comparatively rare. Examples of it are the bitonal passages in the opening of *Tristan*, Act 2 (all horns), the bitonal opening of the compartment scene in *Petroushka* (two clarinets), or the polytonal passages from the Szymanowsky Quartet, Example No. 32, and the Milhaud Symphony, Example No. 33 (all strings).

Spacing and instrumental colour have also a decisive influence on the subjective degree with which our ears perceive the harshness of dissonances. This is best proved when we play piano arrangements of orchestral and choral works. Not only is the variety of tone-colour lost here, and with it its effect of softening the degree of harshness of the various dissonances, but also the spacing of the orchestral texture becomes, for obvious reasons, much narrower. And it is an established fact that the closer dissonant notes are placed to each other the higher becomes their subjective degree of harshness. These are the reasons why orchestral works played on the piano, with its more or less monochrome quality, sound so much more dissonant than when performed in their proper medium.

It goes without saying that what I have remarked on spacing and scoring in respect of works of a predominantly contrapuntal or linear style also holds good for music of a more chordal or vertical nature, as seen in the following example:

No. 36. SCHÖNBERG, *Erwartung.* *

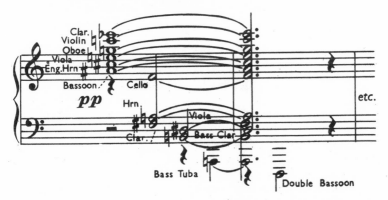

This chord consists of eleven different notes—the most dissonant chord combination imaginable.   But by a special lay-out of the dissonant intervals and a particular way of scoring (choice of readily blending instruments and of their appropriate registers) Schönberg succeeds in smoothing down the harshness of this combination to a very considerable degree.   In modern orchestration such considerations as the heightening and the lowering of the subjective degree of dissonances play a very essential part.

---

* See Schönberg, *Harmonielehre,* pp. 502-3.

III. NEW SCALES

(See also Vol. I, pp. 87-104)

We have discussed some of the devices with which classical tonality was enriched, expanded, and finally broken up. To the array of strong weapons with which the attack was made— increased and intensified chromaticism, free treatment of the unessential notes and the dissonances in general, the splitting up of keys into multiple tonality—we must now add the new scales. Their introduction into the seven-note diatonic system with its two fundamental scales resulted in two forms of tonal development. The first form was its amalgamation with heterogeneous scale systems leading to a hybrid tonality, such as the use of the church modes or the whole-tone scale within the major-minor system. The second was its complete replacement by new scalar systems, such as the microtonal* and the twelve-note scales. Generally speaking, the scales used to such purpose can be divided into two categories: (a) ancient or obsolete scales, such as the church modes, the various scalar systems of European folk-music, and the music of non-European and primitive races; (b) scales, which have been constructed ad hoc by some composers and theoreticians, such as the whole-tone scale, the sixth-tone, quarter-tone, and other microtonal scales. Somehow midway between the two comes Schönberg's twelve-note scale. It grew out of the chromatically intensified diatonic scale and has thus an empirical foundation in the same way as the diatonic scale developed out of the church modes. But in the very fact that Schönberg transformed the empirical chromatic scale into the twelve-note scale—the two are in appearance the same but the functions of their constituent notes greatly different—lies the element of construction.

The tendency to introduce foreign scales or certain of their characteristic steps into the major-minor system goes back to classical music as shown, for instance, in Beethoven's use of the Lydian mode in the adagio section of the third movement of his String Quartet op. 132. With the advent of romanticism and

---

* Tones smaller than a semitone.

the subsequent awakening of national feeling in music, the practice of using scales or characteristic melodic steps peculiar to the folk-music of certain European countries, within the major-minor system became more and more widespread, *viz.*, the music of the national schools in Russia, Bohemia, Scandinavia, Spain and England. As for the use of exotic scales, I said before that it was chiefly the colonial expansion, and through it the closer contact of European musicians with oriental and other non-European music that were responsible for the various forms of exoticism in late romantic and modern music.✻ One has only to recall the influence of exotic music upon the French composers from Felicien David to Debussy and Ravel.

Here are a few examples illustrating the various possibilities of the use of ancient and exotic scales within the diatonic major-minor system.

No. 37. WARLOCK, *Cradle Song.*

This quotation from a song by Peter Warlock is an instance of the archaic use of a church mode. The voice part is in Dorian on G clothed in modern harmony. Another instance is the opening of 'Der Einsame im Herbst' in Mahler's *Lied von der Erde*, with its Dorian mode on D. Bartok's *Bagatelle No. 4* is in Dorian, and *No. I* is cast in modal bitonality (Aeolian and Phrygian). Modal archaism on a large scale is to be found in Pfitzner's opera *Palestrina.* It is also a characteristic feature of the writing of some modern English composers such as Vaughan Williams, Holst, Warlock, Rubbra and others, who have partly based their work on the modal style of the Elizabethan composers.

✻ The phonograph and the gramophone played an important part in this respect. For instance, Puccini, in his *Butterfly* and *Turandot,* used some tunes that he heard in recordings of Japanese and Chinese music.

Among the exotic scales frequently used by European composers are the so-called Gypsy scale C, D, E flat, F sharp, G, A flat, B, C with its two augmented seconds—characteristic of the music in the Balkans and the Near East—and the pentatonic—anhemitonic scale C, D, E, G, A which forms the basis of most music in the Far East. * To European ears this scale is almost a tune in itself which may account for its frequent use at one time.   It is also found in the folk-music of Ireland, Scotland and England, and is, therefore, often encountered in the music of the English folk-song school.   A good example is the fourth movement of Vaughan William's *Pastoral Symphony* where both melody and harmony are partly based on the anhemitonic-pentatonic scale.   The fact that this scale also occurs in the Gregorian Chant has induced some modern composers to use it in works of a religious or biblical character to suggest something archaic, primitive and elemental as did the Swiss composer Burkhard in his recent oratorio *Das Gesicht Jesajas* :

No. 38. BURKHARD, *Das Gesicht Jesajas.*

As for the artificial and specially constructed scales used within the diatonic system of major-minor, the most important among

---

* The pentatonic scale is often described as a " gapped " scale because of the " holes " it shows if compared with the seven-note diatonic scale.   Joseph Yasser, in his *A Theory of Evolving Tonality* (New York 1932), maintains that the seven-note diatonic scale is the product of the fusion of the five regular notes of the pentatonic scale with two auxiliary notes (F and B) which were only used for rapid melodic ornamentation in the manner of passing notes.

them is the whole-tone scale. The view that it is of exotic origin
has so far not been supported by fact. The strict and mechanical
succession of whole tones can only be the result of an experiment.*
The earliest instances of the use of the whole-tone scale are to be
found in Glinka's *Ruslan and Lyudmila* (1842), and Dargomizhsky's
The Stone Guest (1868), where it serves to express something
brutal, uncanny, and frightening. Another early example occurs
in Liszt's *Dante Symphony* where the side-slipping of common
triads on a whole-tone basis evokes the feeling of solemnity and
religious awe. Strauss, in his *Salomé*, uses the whole-tone scale
to the same effect as the Russians (see the passage where Herod
enters, tortured by fears and evil premonitions). Similarly,
Puccini forms the Scarpia motif of his *Tosca* out of a whole-tone
chord progression. The way in which the whole-tone scale may
lead to a succession of augmented instead of perfect triads is
shown by the next example :

No. 39. SCHÖNBERG, *Kammersymphonie*. Op. 9.

The most frequent use of the whole-tone scale occurs in the
music of the French Impressionists where it usually expresses
the mystical and the supernatural as in Debussy's *La Cathédrale
Engloutie* or his *Pelléas et Mélisande*. (For details of the use of the
whole-tone scale in French music, see vol. I, chapter 10.)
    As for the tonality of the whole tone scale, the fact that the
strict equality of its steps deprives the six notes of every mark
of distinction, is responsible for the absence of a central note or
tonic. But it is possible—as modern composers have shown—to
choose one of the six notes as an arbitrary centre and to invest
it, by repetition and frequent return to it, with the function of
a tonal focus. There is only one transposition of the whole-tone

---

** Some musicians trace its origin back to passing notes which fill the whole-tone spaces
between the single notes of an arpeggio of an augmented triad: C-(D)-E-(F sharp)-G
sharp-(A sharp)-C. See, Schönberg, Harmonielehre, pp. 467-68 (3rd Edition).*

scale possible, *i.e.* a semitone higher, so that no matter which of the twelve chromatic notes we take as a starting-point we are always dealing with the same scale either on C or on D flat. Compared with our diatonic system which allows twelve transpositions of the major and minor scales respectively, the scope of the whole-tone scale is infinitely smaller. This and the equality of its steps are liable to create monotony if the scale is frequently used. It is true that the whole-tone scale lent to the music of the French Impressionists new and attractive colours but because of its tonal limitations its effect soon wore off. As with most new scales, the whole-tone scale seems to be most effective if used only sporadically within the diatonic system, and if it enters into functional relations with the latter as, for instance, in Example No. 39, where the succession of whole-tone chords leads to a diminished seventh on A which chord reveals itself as the dominant harmony of E major. Generally speaking, the "spicing" effect of the new scales within the diatonic system is successful in inverse ratio to the frequency of its use.

Of the various new scales suggested and employed by some composers, mention shall be made of a few. Verdi, for instance, whose harmonic language otherwise lacks special interest uses in the "Ave Maria" of his *Quattro Pezzi Sacri* the so-called *scala enigmatica* : C, D flat, E, F sharp, G sharp, A sharp, B, C. The Spanish composer Osca Esplá (b. 1886) has under the influence of native folk-music adopted the scale: C, D flat, E flat, E natural, F, G flat, A flat, B flat. Busoni, partly influenced by experiments carried out by the American Thaddeus Cahill, suggested the division of the whole-tone into six equal parts resulting in a scale of thirty-six notes within the octave. He also advocated various redistributions of the whole and semi-tones in order to arrive at new scale-formations. * Yasser in America worked out a scale with nineteen notes which he calls the supra-diatonic system in which the twelve chromatic degrees are redistributed and separated by intervals of different sizes.** Aloys Hába, Ernest Bloch, John Foulds, the Palestinian composer Mordechai Sandberg and many others have written music in quarter-tones. Yet of all these microtonal scales it may be said that far from having found general acceptance they have as yet remained the "personal and private property"of their inventors.***

---

* *Entwurf einer Neuen Aesthetik der Tonkunst* (Leipzig, 1907).

** *A Theory of Evolving Tonality* (New York, 1932).

*** The idea of writing music in quarter-tones is not so modern as it seems. It actually goes back to the middle of the seventeenth century when it was much discussed in theoretical writings.

IV: THE TWELVE-NOTE SYSTEM

The twelve-note system is perhaps the most artificial and arbitrary system ever conceived by Western musicians. But here again, a natural development prepared the ground. It was the ever-increasing permeation of the diatonic scale by chromatic notes which eventually led to the severing of the few remaining links with the diatonic major-minor system and to the establishment of a functionless chromatic scale as the basis of a new style of writing. The stages of this development were briefly, diatonicism with occasional chromaticism (classical period); diatonicism with gradually increasing chromatic colouring (romantic period); extreme chromaticism on the basis of a chromatically "seasoned" form of the major and minor scales (late romanticism and modern school including the "impure atonalism" of composers such as Bartók, Stravinsky, the early Hindemith, Milhaud, and the Schönberg up to about 1914): and finally twelve-note music based on the chromatic scale in which the five chromatic notes are no longer embellishments, substitutes or functions of the seven diatonic notes, but are all of equal importance and stand in their own right (Schönberg and his atonal school including composers such as Berg, Webern, Wellesz, Pisk and Křenek).

It is true that Schönberg cannot claim priority in the invention of a twelve-note system. For instance, the Frenchman Desiré Paque (b. 1867) traces atonal music back to the beginning of the nineteenth century* and has himself written three atonal violin sonatas about 1911. The Ukrainian composer Jef Golysheff (b. 1895) began to write twelve-note music and even use tone-rows before 1914. And finally the Viennese J. M. Hauer (b. 1883) anticipated Schönberg's tone-rows with his *Tropen*—series of notes which are composed of various arrangements of the twelve chromatic notes. But none of these composers had Schönberg's iron consistency and artistic vision in carrying twelve-note music beyond a purely experimental stage.

It is not my intention to discuss Schönberg's system in all its aspects.** Here our chief concern will be its harmonic or vertical aspect and its "tonality". As to the first point, the

---

* Article, *L'Atonalité ou Mode Chromatique Unique* in *La Revue Musicale*, Ann. 11, 1930.

** For a full discussion of twelve-note music I refer the reader to such excellent writings as Richard Hill's Schönberg's *Tone-rows and the Tonal System of the Future* (Musical Quarterly, January, 1936), Ernst Křenek's *Ueber Neue Musik* (Vienna, 1937), and his recent *Studies in Counterpoint* (New York, 1940), Willy Reich's *Alban Berg* (Vienna, 1937), and the same author's article on twelve-note music in the latest edition of Grove's *Dictionary of Music and Musicians* (London, 1940).

main question is : what are the principles on which chords are built in twelve-note music ? As it was Schönberg's intention to sever every link with traditional harmony, it follows that the principle of chords built by superimposed thirds or fourths had to go by the board. Its place was taken by the new principle of chords built from the *Tonreihe* or tone-row.

Now what is the tone-row ? It is the arrangement of the twelve notes of the chromatic scale in a special order. Every piece has to be based on such a row. To enlarge its scope three variants are derived from it : its inversion, its retrograde form, and its retrograde inversion. All the twelve notes must be used in the order in which they are cast in the row so that as a rule no note can be repeated before the eleven others have been heard. This prevents a note from becoming conspicuous through repetition and thus perhaps assuming the importance of a tonic centre—the very thing to be avoided in this communistic system of twelve equal " comrades ". The row and its three variants can be transposed to all the twelve degrees of the chromatic scale so that a kind of " modulation " is still possible.✱

Now the row can be used both horizontally and vertically. In the latter case we arrive at chords in which the constituent intervals are superimposed in the same order as they occur horizontally in the row. To take an instructive example, Berg's Violin Concerto is based on the following row :

No. 40a. BERG, Violin Concerto.

No. 40b.
Ibid.

✱ In certain Oriental music a somewhat similar system of fixed rows is to be found as in the Indian *raga*, the Arabic *maquam*, and the *weisen* or " modes " of the Jewish Bible cantillations. These are all melodic models which at the same time possess the function of keys in more or less our sense. The transition of a piece from one of these tone-models to another represents a primitive kind of modulation.

The chords in No. 40b are derived from the inversion, transposed a minor sixth up, of the row Example No. 40a. Berg does not keep strictly to the rule of non-repetition of a note before the entire row is heard, as may be seen from Example No. 40b, where the third, fifth and seventh notes of the basic row are repeated in the chords.✸ Berg's row also shows how it is possible, by inventing special rows, to arrive at seemingly tonal chords such as major, minor, diminished, and augmented triads, chords of the seventh and ninth, and so on. But it would go against the very nature of twelve-note music to assign to these chords the tonal function which they would have in music of the diatonic major-minor system.✸✸

It is true that the vertical aspect of the twelve-note music is only of secondary importance. Vertical combinations of intervals are here nearly always the accidental results of linear writing. But is it possible that the composer who writes in this style should not care in the least for the vertical result? Are we to suppose that he does not pay the slightest heed to the varying degrees of harmonic tension which his "accidental" intervals and chords produce? It may have been so when twelve-note music was in its infancy. But later developments show that atonal composers are trying to arrive at certain norms by which to control and check the harmonic elements of their music. It is true that twelve note music *seems* to have abolished the traditional distinction between the consonance and the dissonance. It is also true that though in theory it admits the use of the consonance, twelve-note music deprecates it, and for two reasons.: first, because in the view of the atonal composer consonances create a harmonic standstill—a very debatable point, as according to the theory of the beats (see p. 2) there is, with the sole exception of the octave, no interval of a perfectly consonant nature; and, besides, an interplay of concords and discords will always prevent any such supposed standstill.

✸ It seems that hand- in hand with the further development of twelve-note music and the general perfection of its technical devices go a gradual extension and relaxation of some of its original rules. Křenek, in his *Studies in Counterpoint*, quotes certain instances in which are allowed, not only repetitions of the same note before the entire rôw finishes, but also interruptions of the row by the interpolation of fragments from its derivative forms, the continuation of the row in another but the original part, and even anticipations of notes that (according to their order in the basic row) should enter later.

✸✸ Schönberg felt himself that in place of the former tonal relations which he had abolished something else was needed to hold his music together. This was the tone-row, "a unifying idea which produced not only all the other ideas but regulated also their accompaniment and the chords, the 'harmonies'" (Schönberg in a letter to Nicolas Slonimsky, quoted in the latter's *Music since 1900*, T. M. Dent and Sons, Ltd., 1937).

The second, more plausible reason lies in the tonal implications, which the use of consonant intervals and chords might suggest—the very thing twelve-note music wishes to avoid. This would technically account for the extremely dissonant nature of this style. * What then are those new harmonic norms to which I referred above? It is Křenek's merit to have stated them in his *Studies in Counterpoint*, and to have given us a table in which the various intervals are classified according to their degree of harshness. And lo and behold! twelve-note music adheres, at any rate theoretically, to the same distinction of consonant and dissonant intervals as that found in our traditional text books on harmony. Perfect octaves, perfect fifths, and major and minor thirds, are consonances. Here too, the perfect fourth retains its historical ambiguity (see p. 17) as the question whether it should be regarded as a consonance or a dissonance depends entirely on the context in which this interval occurs.

The new thing, however, in Křenek's classification is his gradation and differentiation of the dissonances unknown to our text-books, in which the dissonances are heaped together in one group, without distinction of their various degrees of harmonic tension. Considering that modern music, particularly that of the twelve-note system, deals primarily with discords, it is only logical that modern composers should be trying to set up a graded scale of dissonances. Here is Křenek's classification:

1. Dissonances of lower tension-degree or "mild" dissonances: major seconds, minor sevenths, and major ninths.

2. Dissonances of higher tension-degree or "sharp" dissonances: minor seconds, major sevenths and minor ninths.

As for the tritone, Křenek considers it a neutral interval dividing as it does the octave into two equal parts. This table enables the composer to differentiate between the various dissonant intervals and thus to use them in a planned and deliberate way. Now if we proceed to compositions of three or more parts, the question arises how to determine the tension-degree of several combined intervals, i.e. chords. Křenek's answer is, that the tension-degree of chords is dependent upon the tension-degree of the intervals which are formed by the constituent notes of the chords themselves. Thus we arrive at a second table in which the chords are classified in the following order of rising tension-degrees:

---

* It is, however, obvious that most of the purely technical features of twelve-note music are only the means by which certain psychological and aesthetic concepts, characteristic of our time, seek to express themselves.

Chords consisting of:

1. Three consonances.
2. Two consonances and one " mild " dissonance.
3. One consonance and two " mild " dissonances.
4. Two consonances and one "sharp " dissonance.
5. One consonance, one " mild ' dissonance, and one "sharp " dissonance.
6. One " mild." and two "sharp " dissonances.

As for three-note chords containing the perfect fourth or the tritone, their character of a dissonance or consonance depends on the third of their constituent notes. Progressions from one group of chords to another will create harmonic tension or relaxation according to the position of the chords in the above table. The composer will thus be able to plan and control crescendos and diminuendos of harmonic tension and use this for formal purposes such as preparation of harmonic climaxes and their subsequent relief.

Křenek's distinction between " mild" and "sharp" dissonances proves that although it treats discords like concords, (that is, discords require no resolution into concords) twelve-note music is still subject to the fundamental psychological law of tension and relaxation of which we spoke in a previous chapter. Yet Křenek makes it clear that this distinction must by no means be taken as absolute. He obviously refers to the modern view of the essentially relative nature of discords and the consequent state of flux and instability in which the modern criteria of the dissonance find themselves when he says that " the decision of what shall be considered a dissonance and how it should be handled is an arbitrary assumption inherent in a particular style, for it depends exclusively on aesthetical concepts " and that " from this catalogue of chords the student may learn nothing more than certain criteria by which to determine tension-degrees of chords in general. He should bear in mind that in practical composition the tension degrees are subject to manifold variations, resulting from the position of the intervals, dynamics, instrumentation, etc. ", and he even warns the student " against pedantry in applying in practical composition the distinction of tension-degrees here explained." Yet despite these qualifications, Křenek's two tables enable us to analyse and judge the harmonic phenomena of twelve-note music with more satisfactory results than it was hitherto possible.

And now for the second important question—the "tonality" of twelve-note music. We must first of all draw a clear distinction between genuine twelve-note music and music that is based upon the chromatic scale which I previously described as the "gingered up" or "seasoned" form of the diatonic major-minor scale. The music of most modern composers belongs to this chromaticized diatonicism, and must therefore be regarded as tonal. For though all the twelve chromatic notes are here continually used, there is still a certain distinction in their functions to be noticed. In spite of a completely free treatment, the five chromatic notes are still regarded as functions of their respective diatonic notes and are consequently closely related to them. Thus tonality is preserved though chromatically expanded to such an extent that, instead of a strong pull, it makes itself felt in a loose gravitational tendency towards a central note, chord, or key.* Considering, however, the great freedom with which the chromatic notes are handled by the modern composer, it will always be extremely difficult and often impossible to establish with any accuracy and beyond ambiguity their true tonal relations. Some of Bartok's *14 Bagatellen* have such chromatically expanded tonality as, for instance, No. 3 (C "major"), No. 6 (B "major"), and No. 10 (C "major"). Similarly, the first of Schönberg's *Drei Klavierstücke* Op. 11 is cast in the key of a chromatically expanded E "major" in which even the tonic note is often replaced by its upper and lower chromatic notes. Many works by Stravinsky, Hindemith, Křenek, and others are based on such intensely chromaticized diatonicism.

From this it is but a logical step to ridding the chromatic notes of their natural connection with their diatonic "parents", to declare them independent, and treat them in their own right as Schönberg has done it. The result is a chromatic scale in which all the twelve notes are equal in importance. There is nothing left to distinguish them from one another in respect of special functions. Consequently, genuine twelve-note music can have no tonal centre and, therefore, no tonality in the accepted sense. Tonality in the accepted sense means the tonality of the seven-note diatonic major-minor system. But if we remember what was said in the first part of this book on a broader conception of tonality, even twelve-note music has its tonality. There I pointed out that the chief criterion for tonality lay in the mere existence of relations of certain notes to a centre, and that consequently modern music has tonality in the sense that certain notes or sequences of notes are given preference over others and thus establish temporary centres which have a decisive bearing on the tonal organisation of the entire com-

---

* In the article on Key, in the supplementary volume to the 4th Edition of *Grove*, a modern Viennese composer is quoted as saying that though his symphony was "in no key at all" yet its "centre was F minor"

position.   Now in Schönberg's *tone-rows* we have these "certain sequences of notes which are given preference over others" and which represent a centre of relationships.   The fact that all the notes occurring in a work in twelve-note technique stand in permanently fixed relations to such a "most favoured" sequence of notes or its three variants constitutes tonality in the broader sense. The "tonic key" is here represented by the particular row upon which the work is based.   Considering the theoretically unlimited number of possible rows, it is obvious that the number of "tonic keys" in twelve-note music is infinite.   But this does not alter the fundamental fact that with the adoption of a row as the basis of a whole composition, this composition becomes tonally fixed and thus achieves tonal coherence.   The term 'atonal' is therefore only true in comparison with classical tonality and is in fact misleading.   Twelve-note music has a different kind of tonal organisation from that belonging to classical tonality, and though it is admittedly artificial and arbitrary it does make for tonal coherence and thus creates a certain sense of musical logic.

This is further borne out by another fact that points to a still retained feeling for key.   It is the transposition of the row and its variants to all the twelve degrees of the chromatic scale to which I referred before.   These transpositions—there are, theoretically speaking, altogether 48 transpositions of one row and its three variants—represent different harmonic zones in the primitive sense of simple changes of pitch.   The transition from the original row—the prime—or its variants to any of their transpositions constitutes a kind of "modulation".   It is particularly when the choice of the transposition "keys" reveals a certain organised plan and direction that we approach the functional modulation of tonal music.   This is the case in Schönberg's latest works (since the Orchestral Variations Op. 31) where the transpositions of rows and their variants are introduced in such a way as to suggest modulations to the "dominant" and "subdominant", in other words, the original row is transposed upwards seven and five semitones respectively, and remains there for some time. Richard Hill, in the article already referred to, quotes the case of Schönberg's *Begleitungsmusik für eine Lichtspielzene* Op. 34, where the opening and the end are in the original row or "tonic key", with typically classical modulations to the "dominant", "subdominant" and "supertonic" in the middle section.   Thus some kind of tonal relation appears to be established and if, as I have remarked, the transpositions occur according to some organised plan it is obvious that they can be used for architectural or formal designs.   It remains to be seen whether this approach to certain harmonic elements of tonal music will be a way out of the *cul-de-sac* in which twelve-note music finds itself at present.

V: HINDEMITH'S CHROMATIC SYSTEM

Schönberg's "communistic" system has been a great stumbling-block for many modern musicians who rightly argue that it goes against the very nature of our sound material. As the harmonic series proves, theirs is a tonal hierarchy based on certain acoustical laws. There are, given a certain note as basis, other notes which stand in varying degrees of relationship to it and through it to each other. It is the varying nature of these relationships that creates this hierarchical order Now Hindemith, in his *Unterweisung im Tonsatz*,* has worked out a new system in which he attempts to reinstate the order of these natural relationships. Like Schönberg's, his system is based upon the chromatic scale but unlike Schönberg's, it possesses a clearly defined organisation of the twelve notes. There are distinct relations between them and it is according to the nature of these relations that the notes assume different melodic and harmonic values, which determine their function in this system. As we shall see presently, the crucial point in Hindemith's chromatic scale is that it belongs neither to the type of " gingered up ". diatonicism nor to Schönberg's twelve-note scale. It may be described as " diatonicised chromaticism " in which the twelve notes now play a similar part to that of the seven in the diatonic system. The following short outline will make this clear.

Unlike Schönberg, Hindemith does not accept the chromatic scale as empirically given, but derives it from the harmonic series. It would lead too far to show in detail the ingenious way in which he arrives at it. But here is the general principle of his method. The first step consists in altering the order of the notes in the harmonic series by moving them one or more points upwards and downwards. The next is to establish their corresponding new fundamentals and to continue this procedure so long until twelve different fundamentals are found, out of which a chromatic row is formed. Take the harmonic series on C :

No. 41

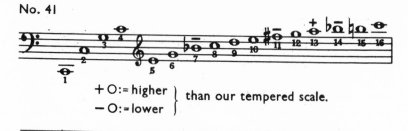

    + O := higher } than our tempered scale.
    − O := lower   }

＊ Schott's Söhne, Mainz, 1937.

Supposing that we move the second overtone C one point down, that is to say, give it the function of a first overtone. It thus becomes the fundamental of a new harmonic series which except for its transposition an octave higher does not differ from the original one. This new fundamental C represents the upper note of the octave within which the other eleven notes shall find their place. We will call it the basic octave. We now proceed to the third overtone G and move it first two points lower or give it the function of a first overtone. Thus G becomes the fundamental of another harmonic series. But as this fundamental lies outside the basic octave it cannot be used. The third overtone is consequently moved one point lower assuming the role of a second overtone. Its corresponding fundamental is then the lower octave G, a note which can be ranged in the basic octave. The next three overtones of the series on C are treated in the same way, the procedure is then reversed the overtones being moved one or more points upwards. The order in which the twelve notes are found is indicated by Hindemith's so-called row No. I.

No. 42. Hindemith's Row No. I.

This order determines the degree of relationship between the central and generating note C and the other eleven notes of the chromatic scale. The further we move from C to the right the lower becomes the degree of this relationship until it reaches zero on F sharp. These varying degrees of relationship in respect of one central note constitute for Hindemith "*Regel und Mass für das Verbinden von Klängen, die Ordnung harmonischer Folgen und dadurch für den klanglichen Ablauf der Komposition*" (rule and measure for the progression of chords, the order of harmonic progressions and, through it, the harmonic course of the composition).

The above row is what has been called a "functional mode."＊ It serves two purposes: like the chromatic scale, it contains all the notes used in this system; yet whereas the chromatic scale

---

＊ This term was first used by Richard Hill in his article on Schönberg's tone-rows where he suggested the following functional mode for diatonic major:

No. 43. Hill's Functional Mode.

or any other scale, for that matter, in which the notes are only arranged according to their pitch, tell us absolutely nothing about their functional significance, the particular arrangement of the twelve notes in Hindemith's row indicates their relation and function in respect of a central note. It is therefore a true functional mode and there is a world of difference between it and Schönberg's row. Hindemith's is a graph showing permanent tone relations and functions as such and has no thematic significance whereas Schönberg's row is a melodic model or a "store of motifs" (Křenek) for practical use in composition.

Hindemith's row No. I gives us, however, only one set of tonal relations, i.e. the relations of the eleven chromatic notes to a centre. But what are the relations between the notes themselves or what is the order of intervals from the point of view of their harmonic value which is dependent· upon their degree of consonance and dissonance? This other set of tone relations is shown in Hindemith's row No. 2 which he derives from the differential notes—a procedure much too complicated to be described in these pages. This second row is nothing else but a table showing the harmonic values of the intervals much in the same way as Křenek's table does (see p. 68)

No. 44. Hindemith's Row No. 2.

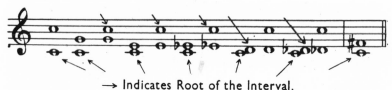

→ Indicates Root of the Interval.

Moving from left to right the intervals become, to use Hindemith's terminology, "less simple" and "less perfect" *(weniger rein)*. Thus the clear distinction between consonant and dissonant intervals is dropped. By drawing no strict line between the seventh and eighth intervals Hindemith takes into full account the modern view of the relative nature of consonant and dissonant intervals. The transition from simple and perfect intervals of no or only slight harmonic tension (the first seven intervals) to less simple and less perfect intervals of higher and highest harmonic tension (the next three intervals) is gradual and steady. The extremes are the octave as the most simple and most perfect and the major seventh as the least simple and least perfect intervals. As for the tritone, like Křenek, Hindemith considers it a neutral interval. Its harmonic value is uncertain and varies according to the context in which it appears.

Now on the basis of this row Hindemith proceeds to build a

system of chords that includes all possible chord formations. The former exclusive principle of building up chords by the super-imposition of thirds is now greatly extended. Fundamental chords may show any combination of equal and unequal intervals, the only distinction being between simple, perfect and less simple, less perfect chords. To determine the degree of their relative simplicity and perfection, row No. 2 must be consulted.

Row No. 2 also plays an important part in regulating chord-progressions. Chords containing relatively simpler and more perfect intervals possess, according to Hindemith, a higher "harmonic value" (Harmonischer Wert) than chords with intervals belonging to the right-hand end of the row. If chords with higher harmonic value move to chords of lower value, the result of such progressions is a harmonic fall (harmonischer Fall), in the opposite case a harmonic rise (harmonischer Anstieg). As the harmonic tension increases in inverse ratio to the harmonic value of the interval or chord, it follows that a step from a "valuable" chord (wertvoller Klang) to a less "valuable" one increases the degree of tension. This crescendo and diminuendo in the har-monic tension, which is treated by the movements of chords of different values, is called the 'harmonic incline' (harmonischer Gefälle). The planning of a balanced and gradual harmonic incline is, according to Hindemith, the purpose and test of good chord progressions unless an abrupt and sudden rise or fall in the har-monic incline is sought for special aesthetic purposes. Thus in the following progression:

No. 45.

the harmonic value of the various chords decreases towards the chord F-A flat -B flat while the harmonic tension increases in proportion. It diminishes again towards the end of the pro-gression at the same ratio as the harmonic value increases. The harmonic incline of this passage is therefore well-balanced. Hindemith argues that by assessing and weighing the harmonic values of chords with the aid of row No. 2, modern composers are given a means by which to control and plan in a very deliberate manner the choice of chords and the harmonic dis-position of a work.

As, however, a chord consists of several different intervals, the question arises which of the several intervals determines its harmonic value. To this Hindemith's answer is that the deter-mining interval is the one with the highest harmonic value, the

" best" interval.   The index for the " best " interval is therefore
again row No. 2.   Thus the respective "best" intervals of the six
chords in the above example are : the perfect fifth C-G, the
major third B flat -D, the perfect fourth E-A, the perfect fourth
F-B flat, the perfect fourth D-G, and finally the perfect fifth C-G.
Consequently the chords Nos. I and 6 have the highest harmonic
value.   Or take the chords of the next example :

No. 46

The " best " interval of the first chord is the perfect fourth D-G,
of the second the perfect fifth C-G.   The first chord possesses
therefore less harmonic value than the second.   Consequently,
the progression from the first to the second chord means a
decrease in harmonic tension.

The next question is how to find the roots of these chords.
As, according to Hindemith, fundamental chords can show any
combination of intervals, it is impossible to determine the roots
of many modern chords such as those of the next example, by
the methods of our traditional text-book harmony which only
recognises chords built up by thirds.

No. 47.

To find the root of a chord it is necessary to establish the root
of its " best " interval which is not always the lower of the two
notes (see row No. 2,.where the roots are indicated by arrows.)
The root of the " best " interval is identical with the root of the
whole chord.   Thus in the above example the " best " interval of
the first chord is the perfect fifth A-E, its root is A which is
therefore the root of the whole chord ; the " best " interval of
the second chord is the perfect fifth C-G, its root is C; consequently,
the root of the whole chord is C.   Similarly the roots of the two
chords of Example No. 46 are G and C respectively, or of the six
chords of No. 45 C, B flat, A, B flat, G, C.   With this method it
is possible to establish the roots of the most complicated chord
formations, formations that are completely unknown to traditional
text-book harmony.

By way of conclusion, a few words must be said on the manner in which Hindemith tackles the problem of tonality. I pointed out before that the basic fact in his system is the 'diatonicized chromaticism', that is to say, every one of the twelve chromatic notes stands in a functional relation to a central note similar to the way in which the seven diatonic notes of the modes and the major-minor scales are related to a tonic. Hindemith maintains that it is thus possible to establish in terms of twelve chromatic keys the tonality of any kind of modern music including pure twelve-note music, as he tries to show in his analysis of a few bars from Schönberg's *Klavierstück Op. 33a*. His method is, roughly, this: he, first of all, establishes the root of a given chord progression as described on p. 76. The line that is formed by this succession of roots *(Stufengang)* shows a variety of different intervals out of which you select, with the aid of row No. 2, the "best" interval. Its root is the tonic note of the whole pro-gression. Take the progression of Example No. 45. The roots of the six chords form the following line:

No. 48

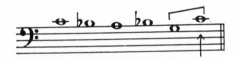

with the perfect fourth G-C as its "best" interval. Its root is C, and this note is consequently the central note to which the six chords must be related. The tonality of the whole progression is a chromatic C "major". In dealing with longer sections and whole movements, however, a variety of other points has to be considered, points that fall outside the scope of this book.

My aim has merely been to give a very rough outline of Hinde-mith's system as far as it bears on harmonic and tonal problems. It is admittedly very complicated and abstruse. But it represents a serious and thought-provoking attempt to bring about a fusion, at any rate theoretically, between the functional system of tonal music and pure chromaticism. And it tries to introduce order and organisation into the chaotic state in which the theory of modern music still finds itself. As such it deserves the attention and serious consideration of every musician who cares for the vital problems of his art.

POSTCRIPT

To follow the trends of contemporary harmony with its currents and cross-currents, its wealth of new phenomena, its freedom from traditional rules and limitations is a fascinating study. But it is also a bewildering one. Bewildering because the harmonic thoughts of to-day are in a constant flux. All that we can say with any certainty is that harmony and tonality are passing through a period of fermentation. The position to-day is not dissimilar to that at the turning-point of the sixteenth century. Then the tonal basis of music changed from the modes to the major minor system and, at the same time, the style of writing turned from the horizontal to the vertical. To-day we are witnessing the supersession of the major-minor tonality by various other systems of which the twelve-note system occupies the centre of the contemporary stage. The style of writing has also changed but this time from the vertical to the horizontal. Where will it all lead to? Is the musician of the present day, standing as he does in the very vortex of these changes, able to see a path ahead that promises to lead to firmer ground? Is he justified in assuming that this present welter of ideas and tendencies may once again crystallize into a new "classical" system with a firm tonal basis and with clearly defined and well-ordered relations of its melodic and harmonic elements? It is perhaps bold to put this question at the present juncture and try to answer it. But there are certain signs in the most recent course of modern music that seem to point in that direction. I have mentioned them before without, however, interpreting them in this light. What they all seem to have in common is that they suggest a deliberate approach to certain points of the classical tone-system. These signs are, first of all, the attempts of some modern musicians to set the house of dissonances in order by grading and classifying them according to their respective degrees of harshness. Next, there is the tendency in more recent twelve-note compositions to plan the various transpositions of the row and its variants in such a manner that the different harmonic zones, thus formed, stand to each other in relations that remind one of those of the key-schemes in tonal music. Moreover, atonal composers are inventing special rows in which the constituent notes are so arranged as to imply tonal harmonies. For instance, Alban Berg, in his Violin Concerto, invented such a row (see Examples Nos. 40 a and b) and used it vertically to suggest tonal chords. And finally, there is Hindemith's attempt to set up a system on the basis of a functional chromatic mode with clearly defined relations between the twelve notes.

It seems that modern musicians have grown out of the iconoclastic stage and are beginning to plan a new organisation of the sound-material in the light of past experiences. But will it be a completely new order? Will it contain none of the elements of the classical tone-system which after all was the basis of Western music during the last three centuries and to which the tonal evolution of the preceding period of over six hundred years seems to have been but a preparation? It cannot be that the music of fifty or a hundred years hence will have completely discarded the fundamental facts of the classical system. We cannot get away from the laws of nature. Nature has given us the phenomenon of the harmonic series containing in its first six notes—the most important of the whole series—the major triad. The major triad existed before the first musician was born and it will go on existing after the last musician has left this planet. The classical system is based upon the major triad and its closest derivative, the minor triad. That is why the common triad will always be the clearest symbol of tonality, and that is why the classical system is the most natural and, hence, the most organic of all conceivable tone-systems. It has, of course, its limitations as I have tried to show when I gave the reasons for suggesting a broader conception of tonality. After all, art is not a mere imitation of nature. Were it so, polyphonic music would have never risen from its primitive state of *organa* and fauxbourdons. Instinct, experiment, trial and error have all combined to lead the adventurous spirit of the Western musician to the realisation of the inherent horizontal and vertical possibilities of the harmonic series. Thus he came to create the *art* of music. Yet the wonderfully organic growth of Western music during the past five centuries was essentially conditioned by its natural tonal basis. So great and towering had the edifice become that we could no longer see the simple but firm foundation on which it stood. But it seems that after a period of uncertainty and of many experiments modern musicians are beginning to rediscover this natural foundation. It is dawning upon us that in the tone-system to come, the basic element of the major triad and all that it implies will have to find its place, too, if this system is to prove of intrinsic value. This does not mean going back to the simple diatonic major-minor and trimming it with a few modern devices as had been done in the 'neo-classical' music of some years back. True, the possibilities of the major-minor are exhausted. So are those of chromaticism of diatonic origin. And as for pure chromaticism, twelve note music has so far not been much more than a fascinating experiment, and, will remain so as long as it flouts the implications of the harmonic series. But the evolutionary spiral has not broken. We seem to be at the beginning of what I called "diatonicized chromaticism'—an amalgam of the functional elements of tonal music with the chromaticism of twelve-note music. If these two grow into an organic whole—and the signs I mentioned seem promising—then the music of the future will have the tonal clarity and logic of the classical system, and the freedom and wide range of expression that pure chromaticism gives.

BIBLIOGRAPHY

Abraham, Gerald   :   *A Hundred Years of Music*, 1938
                          This Modern Stuff (2nd Ed.), 1939

Andrews, Hilda   :   *Modern Harmony*, 1934

Barnes, A. F.   :   *Practice in Modern Harmony*, 1937

Bauer, Marion   :   *Twentieth Century Music*, 1933

Busoni, Ferrucio   :   *Entwurf einer Neuen Aesthetik der Tonkunst*, 1907

Casella, Alfredo   :   *L'Evoluzione della Musica* (Also in English), 1924

Coeuroy, André   :   *La Musique Française Moderne*, 1924
                          Panorama de la Musique Contemporaine, 1928

Dumesnil, René   :   *La Musique Contemporaine en France*, 1930

Dyson, George   :   *The New Music*, 1924

Eimert, Herbert   :   *Atonale Harmonielehre*, 1924

Gray, Cecil   :   *A Survey of Contemporary Music*, 1924

Hauer, J. M.   :   *Vom Wesen des Musikalischen*, 1920
                      Zwölftontechnik, 1925

Hindemith, Paul   :   *Unterweisung im Tonsatz*, 1937

Hull, A. E.   :   *Modern Harmony*, 1918

Křenek, Ernst   :   *Ueber Neue Musik*, 1937
                       Studies in Counterpoint, 1940

Kurth, Ernst   :   *Die Voraussetzungen der Theoretischen Harmonik*, 1913
                      Grundlagen des Linearen Kontrapunkts, 1927

Lambert, Constant :   *Music Ho!* 1934

Lenormand, René :   *A Study of Twentieth-Century Harmony*, 1915
                       (2nd Ed. 1940)

McNaught, W. S.   :   *A Short Account of Modern Music and Musicians*, 1937

Mersmann, Hans : *Musik der Gegenwart*, 1923
                  Die Moderne Musik seit der Romantik, 1928

Myers, Rollo H. : *Modern Music*, 1923

Nüll, Edwin v.d. : *Moderne Harmonik*, 1932

Pannain, Guido : *Modern Composers*, 1932

Schönberg, Arnold : *Harmonielehre*, (3rd Ed.) 1921

Weissmann, Adolf : *The Problems of Modern Music*, 1925

Yasser, Joseph : *A Theory of Evolving Tonality*, 1932

Articles on Harmony, Key, Tonality, etc., in Grove's *Dictionary of Music and Musicians*, Riemann's *Musik-Lexikon*, Cobbett's *Cyclopedic Survey of Chamber Music*, Scholes, *The Oxford Companion to Music*, and in periodicals including *Music & Letters*, *The Musical Times*, *Monthly Musical Record*, *The Musical Quarterly*, *Modern Music*, *La Revue Musicale*, *La Rassegna Musicale*, *Musica d'Oggi*, *Die Musik*, *Musikblätter des Anbruch*, *Der Auftakt*.

INDEX OF MUSICAL ILLUSTRATIONS

INDEX OF COMPOSERS AND WORKS